I0738009

GONE IN OCTOBER

LAST REFLECTIONS ON JACK KEROUAC

Also by
John Clellon Holmes

Go

The Horn

Get Home Free

Nothing More to Declare

The Bowling Green Poems

Death Drag: Selected Poems 1948 – 1979

Visitor: Jack Kerouac in Old Saybrook

Interior Geographies

Gone in October: Last Reflections on Jack Kerouac

Dire Coasts

Displaced Person: The Travel Essays

Representative Men: The Biographical Essays

Passionate Opinions: The Cultural Essays

Night Music: Selected Poems

GONE IN OCTOBER

LAST REFLECTIONS ON JACK KEROUAC

John Clellon Holmes

LIMBERLOST PRESS
2022

ACKNOWLEDGMENTS

Grateful acknowledgment is given to the following magazines where some of these works originally appeared: *Moody Street Irregulars*, *Stony Hills*, *Playboy*, and *The Review of Contemporary Fiction.*

"The Great Rememberer" first appeared in *Nothing More to Declare* (E. P. Dutton, 1967).

The title essay, "Gone in October," originally published in *Playboy* in 1973, won the magazine's "Best Nonfiction Award" for that year.

"Envoi in Boulder," which appears as the last essay in John Clellon Holmes' *Representative Men: The Biographical Essays* (University of Arkansas Press, 1988), is a revised and embellished version of "Tender Hearts in Boulder," which first appeared in *The Review of Contemporary Fiction* and later in the 1985 Limberlost Press edition of *Gone in October.*

Cover photograph of John Clellon Holmes and Jack Kerouac, Old Saybrook, Connecticut, early-1960s, by Shirley Holmes.

The 1985 edition of *Gone in October* comprised Nos. 14 & 15 of *The Limberlost Review.*

Layout and book design: Meggan Laxalt Mackey,
Studio M Publications & Design, Boise, Idaho.

ISBN 978-0-578-36013-3

Published by:

Rick and Rosemary Ardinger, Editors
17 Canyon Trail, Boise, Idaho 83716
www.limberlostpress.com

Dedicated to
Rick and Rosemary
for friendship and belief

CONTENTS

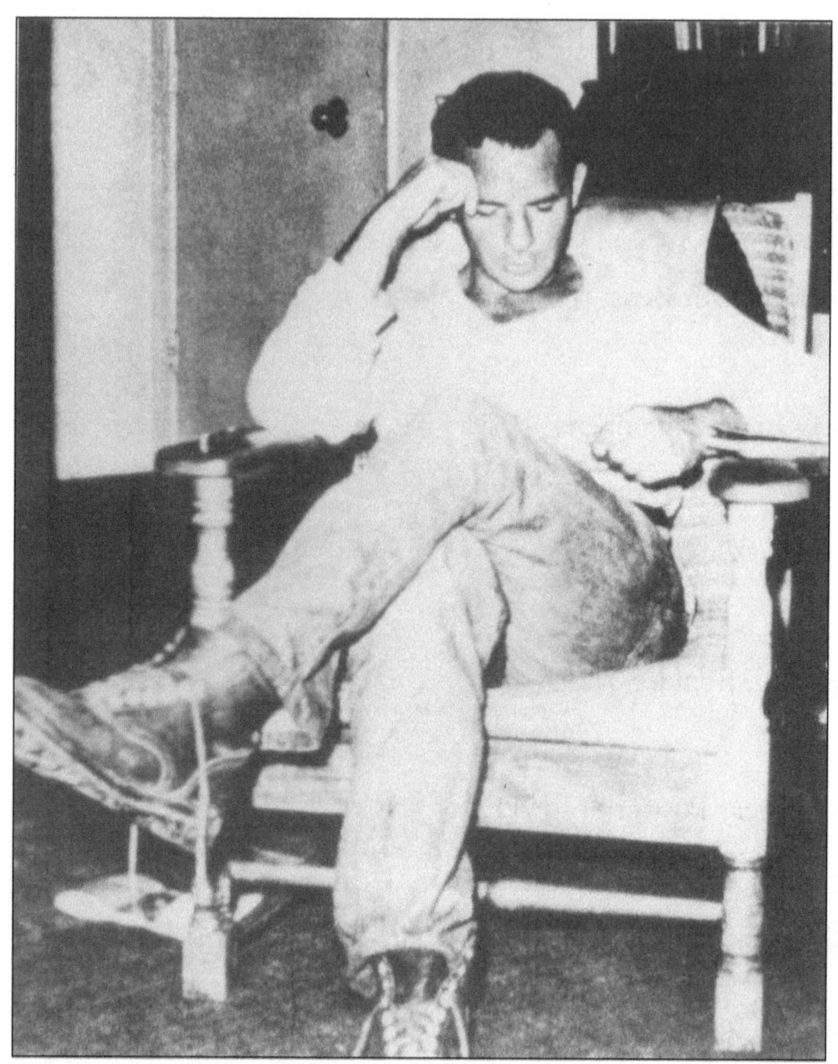

Kerouac, 1951. Photo by Carolyn Cassady.

GOING WEST ALONE

—for Jack

Jack's marrow-old in this old world,
an old soul, a leathered Chinese hobo
thrashing down in the river-marshes,
down there in the vast hush of dusk.
Mostly these days he wants to tipple,
speculate and unthink in solitude.
He has left the world already, so he putters.
This oldness in him burdens me—
sobering as an omen of our common end.
Odd that no one hears the old man in him,
sniffing for eternity in railroad-weeds,
a foretaste of his death in town-edge twilights.

It is painful for me to think of him
in his San Francisco Third Street room.
It is so real to me, and so unreachable.
The imagined-moment has the quality
of something having absolutely happened.
He's passing through the seven stages
of consciousness so fast, so young,
most of us have never even noticed.
I think of him with his cat in the woods,
down by the river-marge—cooking, humming,
sleeping sound as he does, then moving on.
I think of how avid he has hungered in this world,
passing out of it. I know his window.
He knows I know, and carefully
we never speak of wisdom anymore.

—1964

INTRODUCTION

John Clellon Holmes and Jack Kerouac, early-1960s, Old Saybrook, Connecticut. Photograph by Shirley Holmes.

THE DEATH OF A CLOSE FRIEND slams a door in the face. It seems the cruel and final sundering of a shared-life, and if that dead friend has been an important comrade (in more than just affection), small and subtle severings occur after the big one, as that friend's hold on the mind as well as the heart gradually loosens. So it was with the death of Jack Kerouac for me.

This book collects all my writing about him. It seemed proper to include among the posthumous essays the only extended piece I ever wrote about him while he was alive. That piece, "The Great Rememberer," was part of the book, *Nothing More to Declare* (Dutton, 1967). It had been written in 1965 and sent to him for correction or objection. His only quibble (caught only after the book appeared) was that I had described his eyes as brown whereas in fact they were blue. I have amended the reference here. I think he was hurt that I hadn't noticed. But at the first reading in typescript he felt "as if soothed and balmed by a Great Defender, and justified, at last, for once" (Letter: August 25, 1965). I have reprinted the piece second in the sequence here.

The three other essays in this book are the post-mortem effects of his abrupt death in 1969, which ended our 22-year-long friendship. They were written at varying degrees of distance from that autumnal event, and concern different aspects of my relationship to his memory. The four essays are presented in the following order: his heritage, his life and work, his death and funeral, and his legacy.

The first, "Rocks in Our Beds," was undertaken at the request of Arthur and Kit Knight for a special issue of the Maine-based review, *Stony Hills*, which they edited in the spring of 1981. It was their notion that I might be able to throw some light on the influence of New England in Kerouac's work. I had never given the matter much thought, and in the process of doing so I discovered as much about the power of that influence on myself as on Jack. It was the discovery of yet another bond between us, one that had shaped our attitudes towards Time and our individual lives.

Then comes the aforementioned "The Great Rememberer."

The title-piece (which is next), somewhat shorter than here, was published in *Playboy* in 1973, and was based on a much longer journal-entry made immediately after returning from Jack's funeral. It was an attempt to establish the hard facts of that event (including the inner facts) as I knew them, the most surprising of which was the first glimpse of what Kerouac had meant to strangers and the general culture, and my personal response to this new awareness. The last piece, "Tender Hearts in Boulder," published in *The Review of Contemporary Fiction* in 1983 [revised here as "*Envoi in Boulder*"], is a report on the Naropa celebration of the quarter century since the appearance of *On the Road*. By that time, though Kerouac had been mythologized in biography and rumor, for the dozen or so of his friends whom Allen Ginsberg brought together in Colorado in July of 1982, the conference was more of a fraternal than a literary occasion, the trigger for private reflections as much concerned with the future as with the past. It signaled an ending to the old life with which Kerouac had been associated, and for me at least a final turning of the key in the door that had slammed shut thirteen years before.

The non-sequential order of the pieces as presented is deliberate, because each deals with a separate repositioning (middle distance, closeup, long shot, fade-out) in the slow laying-of-the-ghost that death initiates. That process in me, the long saying-of-goodbye, is completed with this book. Having cooperated with a horde of biographers, critics, correspondents and interviewers over the years, now—in the raw foothills of the Ozarks, in this wet spring of 1984—what unknowingly began on the flooded Pemigewasset River, under the hard gaze of the White Mountains, in the equally wet spring of 1937, comes to an end at last, and the ghost in my mind can rest.

—John Clellon Holmes

Jack Kerouac, 1956. Photo from the jacket of On the Road, *by William Eichel.*

First books: The Town and The City (1950) with dust jacket photo of Kerouac, and GO (1952) with dust jacket photo of Holmes.

ROCKS IN OUR BEDS

Young boys: Jack Kerouac (left) and John Clellon Holmes. Photo of Kerouac courtesy family photo archive. Photo of Holmes courtesy Lila Dizefalo.

My heart is heavy as lead
because the blues have spread
rocks in my bed.
—Duke Ellington

ELECTIVE AFFINITIES, CORRESPONDENCES, ANALOGIES. Oh, New England, how you curse your scribblers with a double-view! The autumn twilight haunted by burnt August in the wood smoke; skeletal treeshadows on virgin snow in the piercing clarity of winter-sun; the loosening loam and early budlets of hesitant, pastel spring; the summers, languid and a-buzz and brief, tinged with the foreknowledge of the red and yellow withering to come—in such seasonal places the senses are poised, keen, made avaricious by the imminence of change. The imagination smoulders, flares, dies, only to flare again. And boys in attic rooms in redbrick factory towns, or in the kerosene kitchens of upland farms, or in sight of deep water in the Bostons and New Bedfords of the region, sit up late, alone, and one night start to write. New England, oldest and most homely of American places—it's what's fleeting and elusive in you that demands words! The centuries-old redbrick towns and upland farms remain, but the scribbling boys are stabbed by a premonition of their own mortality. Time, as inevitable as December, drives them on, and all too often away.

I was one of those ruminative boys, Kerouac was another; Olson, Creeley, Weiners—still others. New England's stony fields and twisting streets, which had bred the earliest American literature, bred us too. Later, we would decamp for the New Yorks, Mexico Cities, Friscos, and Londons of the vast and morally ambivalent world beyond, but New England, a mere postage stamp on the immense envelope of modern consciousness, was nevertheless stamped, uncancelled, on our imaginations. To the critics, we were all wanderers— the flotsam of cities, jazz, dope, and psychic anarchy. Actually, we were seeking to align the phantom vision and the factual reality of that double-view, and the tap-root in us (what Lawrence called "the spirit of place") wouldn't pull: It had ensnarled itself in the inhospitable soil of Massachusetts, New Hampshire, Maine, and Connecticut. And it held.

On the banks of the flood-choked Pemigewasset River in Plymouth, New Hampshire, in 1937, I stood in muddy shoes, with a paperbagful of doughnuts just tonged out of the grease by our half-Algonquin cook, Dorothy, watching with awe as upwrenched trees sailed seaward, and the pilings of the bridge to Holderness stood stubborn and spanless in the boiling surge, and knew the dawning of a first awareness—this was a world-in-time! Rushing heedlessly around us, into us, through us! And I had no words to deal with the perception, and thereby discovered the reality, and the necessity, of words. I ached to build pilings that would withstand the flood in me.

Downriver a few days later, beyond where the Pemigewasset flowed into the Merrimack, Kerouac watched those same trees quickeningly borne under the Moody Street Bridge in Lowell on their way to that most austere of seas, the North Atlantic, and perhaps first heard the dire *mwee-hee-hee* of Dr. Sax echo in the roar beneath his shoes. We would discover this eerie correspondence in our lives only years later in New York, up way past midnight, the river of traffic in the clashing street below roaring as loud as the converging rivers of our boyhood, and bringing the memory back to both of us in the same instant.

Oddly, though we were associated with New England all our writing-lives, both of us having written novels about it, Kerouac and I were outlanders there. Though we had both been born in Massachusetts (at opposite ends of the state), I had spent much of my childhood in New Jersey, California and Long Island, and Jack was of French Canadian stock, and was always dogged by a dark sense of foreignness. Yet we both felt New England in us, as if it was a mother-place, spectral with *deja vu*. Through all his perigrinations, his many temporary homes, Jack longed for a cabin in the deep woods of New Hampshire, or for the cozy kitchens of Lowell. It was the one ghost-hope that never left him. For myself, after ten years of city-life had started to corrode my nerves, I instinctively moved to a ramshackle house in Connecticut, took to the saws and hammers, and made a home at last.

Once, during one of his spells of desperate spiritual homesickness, when the cabin-vision was upon him like a claw on his forehead, Jack wrote to me: "Oh, John, Alack, a John, John a dreams, I'll be Thoreau to your Emerson." Elective affinities again. Literature, like a gravestone-rubbing, laid over life until the shadow-image and the substance of the stone were one, words at once approximate to the granite that had endured and the person lying under it who hadn't, except as a name, a scrap of scripture, and the dates. The source of our awareness of time and eternity was in the handsawn clapboards that had withstood a hundred raging Novembers, and in the old bricks behind which all the Dickensian looms had long gone silent, and in the impersonal sea on which no whaler, trawler or merchantman had ever left a mark to indicate that they had set out, and somehow gotten back, and set out again, and one day not returned. We lived with this as we lived with the seasons. All voyages, like all youths, all summers, all vaulting hopes, end in the ambiguity of the Pequod stoven-in as much by Ahab as by Moby Dick.

Kerouac's immodest analogy between the Concord writers and ourselves was natural to the likes of us, though it was somewhat inaccurate. Like Emerson, he had a taste for the arcane and mystical; like Thoreau, I had an equal taste for logic and clarity. He was given to pithily-stated apothegms like Emerson. I tended to see things, Thoreau-like, in terms of irony. Like Emerson, Jack was notorious in his time, a freshet of hints that undammed other men. I sank quickly and quietly into an obscurity not unlike Thoreau's. Both of us, like them, eventually looked to the East. In our different ways, we were Transcendentalists. I beat out my exile in the suffocating cities, and became a countryman—a reasonably good carpenter, electrician and recluse. Jack never made it, and remained psychologically displaced and physically uprooted until it killed him. Both of us had a taste for the local, and for locality, but when we were together in New England, he and I, we never felt the need to speak of the place. We didn't enthuse over quaint houses, mittened winters, waterfront taverns, Scollay Square when it was sordid and exciting, brown doilied parlors, icy nosetips, furnace ashes on the stoops, hard cider with a prickle in it, the primitive content to be found in blazing fireplaces, the smell of damp books in plain stone libraries, April's uprush in the throat—it all just came back, the dust-covers on the furniture of these memories snatched off in an instant, and we knew we need not explain anything to each other about—well, all that.

But it was New England that spoke in *Doctor Sax*, where all the coagulated evil in the world gathers like a cosmic boil, and then bursts into a husk of doves. Equally, it was New England that drove my Old Man Molineaux (in *Get Home Free)* to struggle against his kedge anchor, hungering after wild places, only to collapse at the end, capitulant and secretly relieved, having experienced them all in his imagination anyway. In New England, speculation is no farther away than the woodpile, spiritual bliss comes to the swinger-of-birches.

So we were subtlely different than Ginsberg or Burroughs or Corso in our crowd. We wore a sense of the past like a birthmark. Indians skulked our dreams. Guilt, like the evening cry of a loon over a sinister, fir-girt lake, guilt for the truths we had believed in and failed to find, encouraged in us a fatal premonitory sense. Still, I was privately proud of the name of the bad versifier that I bore, and Jack was pursued all his life by a feeling that an unknown heritage was his—but from whom? He never stopped trying to search out his enigmatic lineage. Allen (from New Jersey) and Bill (from St. Louis) and Gregory (from Lower New York) never felt this strong pull backwards, not alone to family, but to place, to continuum, to a tradition of mind constantly in need of freshening. Time was the ghost behind the woodwork for Jack and me, and in our inmost natures we believed, despite rapturous or desperate asserverations to the contrary, that he who fights time can only lose. We were Transcendentalists with hangovers—that was the difference. We had moral rocks in our beds.

We liked the great Russian novelists because of New England. We were no strangers to cramped rooms, cold streets, extremes of introspection. We were at home with Zen Koans and "dark nights of the soul" when they came to us, having read Emily Dickinson and William James. The ambiguities of puritan fervor and pagan fever entered us with Hawthorne, reaching an ultimate pitch in Herman Melville, an outsider in New England himself, in whose work language struggles to at once contain and release the intuitive knowledges that lie buried beneath all intellection.

The bed's a place for dreams, and rest, and love—a private place. But our beds were like New England's stony fields. You had to work hard before you could dream in them, much less hope. You piled the stones into fences, you dug and heaved and dragged at them in all weathers, raging, despairing, intent, all alone at the task, but always brooding on more than the task-because you knew the fences would outlast you. Kerouac played phantom baseball games in his upstairs room; I deployed armies of lead soldiers in battles as complex as Waterloo. But as we played them, we mused far beyond these callow games, and early on we both began to write away the psychological bruises of nights spent in those rocky beds. Robert Frost found in the day's toil out of doors the proper stuff for the evening's poems—but what austere and metaphysical bucolics they were! Melville found a fatal image in a fish. Just as Kerouac did in a milltown and its river, baldly deeming his account of it, *Faust Part Three.* And I saw in a reprobate old boozer all our secret hopes for heaven. We were religious men without a creed.

I could always drive a nail straight, and liked the same clean thwack in a line of poetry. Olson knew that a poem and a porch stood up for the same reasons. Jack's litmus-paper consciousness recorded the destiny, as well as the immediacy, of all sensations. Even our lyrical effusions, our vernal affirmations, were somehow autumnal too. Prodigality and thrift, excess and ascetism, hope and despair, warred not only in our world, but in our very natures. That was the New England view—commonplace and dooming as Eve's McIntosh, as mysterious as the sweet syrup prisoned in the wintertree.

The restlessly-speculative nature achieves no certainties, no home port. Thoreau moved from Walden Pond, Henry Beston from the Outermost House. Melville ended up on 26th Street in New York as obscure as Kerouac in Florida. For New Englanders handle fame badly. It never corresponds to the sort of spiritual eminence they're after. They look over their shoulders or down at their feet when praised, as if the praiser hadn't glimpsed what

might be truly praiseworthy, and cheapens praise by easy praising. Suspicious of groups, movements and messiahs, the New England writer knows that below the fumy brain is the importunate heart, and below that the sap that spring draws up into the loins, and below that the dumb feet planted on rock, and beneath the rock—clay. It is a view that sees the human being as the fragile circuit between heaven and earth, life as a limbo-state, and literature the record of a passage through the continual dissolution of forms into other forms, the clearing of a field. I think that those of us, who were from New England and became associated with the so-called Beats, brought this subtlely different double view to their concerns. Hindu *fakirs* lie on beds of nails, the spirit conquering matter itself. But we had abstract rocks in our beds, and our nights and our lives were troublous with their haulage. "Go moan for man," Kerouac said, and his work was just such an outcry and a lamentation. Olson's enormous construct, *Maximus*, glimpsed all the world and all of time in Gloucester, just as Thoreau had done in Concord. My own work attempted to express a certain edge of fond skepticism about appearances, and a stubborn feeling for the heart that beats beneath our masquerades, which, as I've gotten older, seems the only part of wisdom on which I'll stand.

So, New England, you taught us to find the blessing in the curse you laid on us; you accustomed us to gales and sometimes perishing in them; you gave us a taste for things that are homely and well made; you fashioned us into a peculiar breed—gloomy, speculative, always wrestling with that urgent poetry that only life-and-death-keyed people feel choking up in them, travelers whose wanderings are only circuitous routes of return.

Beyond the last league of the last sea is New Bedford again. Or the grave. Robert Lowell was heading for Back Bay when his life gave out. Jack's back in Lowell now. We New England writers of this time sold our wooden nutmegs to the world, and some of us have lived to see them prized as artifacts. Who knows? Perhaps that was the intention all along. To see the spirit in the meanest of things. For after the night, is light. Then dark again. But that new dark is peopled, and the field less rock-strewn than before.

Jack Kerouac, circa 1958.

THE GREAT REMEMBERER

Jack Kerouac, Northport, Long Island, New York, July 1960. Photo by John Clellon Holmes.

"A GREAT REMEMBERER REDEEMING LIFE from darkness": thus Kerouac, self-described. But he is, as well, an American phenomenon as indigenous as a gas station in the Grand Canyon: the athlete-artist, the tramp transcendentalist, the renowned recluse. And despite all the public nonsense about "the King of the Beats," he remains as unique, primal and obscure as Niagara Falls, which has been looked at so often it can no longer be seen.

Though he has already created a larger body of work than any of his contemporaries, to most people his name summons up the image of a carefree do-nothing sensation-hunter. Though that body of work creates a dense, personal world that is as richly detailed as any such American literary world since Faulkner, he is continually thought to be nothing but the poet of the pads and the bard of bebop. And though he is a prose innovator in the tradition of Joyce, whose stylistic experiments will bear comparison with any but the most radical avant-gardists of the century, he is constantly ticketed as some slangy, hitchhiking Jack London, bringing a whiff of marijuana and truck exhaust into the lending libraries. In short, the kind of writer that only America could produce, and that only America could so willfully misunderstand. One has only to remember Melville "the writer of boys' sea stories" and Whitman "the author of 'O Captain My Captain'" to recognize what legacy of national neglect Kerouac has fallen heir to. For ours is a benevolent society. Not for us to doom our Mark Twains to a garret. No, instead we praise them as vaudevillians. And later wonder why they gnashed their teeth.

The life "redeemed from darkness," which Kerouac's books describe, is nothing less than the whole of his actual life, and if the man (and it's the man I am concerned with here) can be approached through the work, it is primarily because that work is not so much concerned with events as it is with consciousness, in which the ultimate events are images. A montage of that consciousness might unreel like this:

Redbrick alleys of New England. Brown 1930's suppertimes. Loam-rank cellars full of shadows. The boom of sneakers on track-meet boards. Love's choked throat under the wheeling prom lights.

Times Square wartime bars. Hip sneers in neon flicker. October intersections, Butte midnights, Denver glooms. The awesome prairie from a fatalistic truck. Generation parties whooped on beer. Wino flophouse mattresses. Lost reds of twilight on Mexico adobe walls. A junkie's crucifix. Intersections, further intersections. Pacific immensities by the kerosene cabin. Mad hobos of rainy Susquehannas. Then all of it again. Intersections, lofts, bars, woodsy musings. Until God is no more a superstition, and Truth lies in the Buddha's blessed emptiness, and our portion is to moan for man, and meanwhile wait.

That is the burden of the consciousness that invests Kerouac's books (sixteen so far), and to read them straight through leaves you exhausted, bowed-down, baffled, roused, depressed, exulted, riled, amused but above all *silenced*—silenced by that immensity of distance and that eternity of time, which most religious visions and all hallucinogenic drugs hint at as the true nature of Reality. An odd emotion stirs in your throat, the emotion you would experience if, from some great height, you saw a lone figure walking across an empty plain in the dusk. A pang of creatureliness, intensified by awe, would reconcile you at the exact moment that it saddened. Or as Kerouac puts it, daring to use those orphaned accents that actually murmur behind most modern bravado:

> "I'm writing this book because we're all going to die—In the loneliness of my life, my father dead, my brother dead, my mother far away, my sister and my wife far away, nothing here but my own tragic hands that once were guarded by a world, a sweet attention, that now are left to guide and disappear their own way into the common dark of all our death, sleeping in me raw bed, alone and stupid: with just this one pride and consolation: my heart broke in the general despair, and opened up inwards to the Lord, I made a supplication in this dream."

That paragraph could stand as the key to the man. But what sort of man is he? Though few modern writers have embedded themselves more solidly in their books, there is far more to Kerouac than the books suggest, and I have to admit to the difficulties of my writing about him, so much is my adult life entangled in our friendship.

He has awed me with his talents, enraged me with his stubbornness, educated me in my craft, hurt me through indifference, dogged my imagination, upset most of my notions, and generally enlarged me as a writer more than anyone else I know. We have wrangled, and yelled, and boozed, and disliked, and been fond of one another for almost twenty years. He has figured in my books, sometimes directly on the page, but most often standing just off it; and I appear here and there in his, under various names, though usually as a snide, more fortunate, migraine-headache intellectual, who borrows his ideas, makes money from his perceptions, and is always trying to involve him in stifling ego dramas. And yet only one part of his complicated nature thinks of me this way. For the rest of it, we are curiously close. We represent something to one another: everything we are *not* ourselves.

Our minds, which work in opposite ways, have never been entirely compatible. He is freely contradictory, I tend to be trapped by my own consistencies; he absorbs, I analyze; he is intuitive, I am still mostly cerebral; he muses, I worry; he looks for the perfection in others, and finds existence flawed; I am drawn *toward* the flaw, and believe in life's perfectability. But there is, and was from the beginning, a real and generous affection between us, based on a peculiar sense of kinship—puzzling, maddening, indescribable—that has made our relationship oddly fateful for both of us. For his part of it, I think he believes my heart is in the right place, but I bore him after a while. For mine, what follows may suggest a little of what he has meant to me.

We became friends more quickly than I have ever become friends with anyone else. Everything about him was engaging in those days. He was open-hearted, impulsive, candid and very handsome. He didn't seem like any other writer that I knew. He wasn't wary, opinionated, cynical or competitive, and if I hadn't already known him by reputation, I would have pegged him as a poetic lumberjack, or a sailor with Shakespeare in his sea locker. Melville, armed with the manuscript of *Typee*, must have struck the Boston Brahmins in much the same way. Stocky, medium-tall, Kerouac had the tendoned forearms, heavily muscled thighs and broad neck of a man who exults in his physical life. His face was black-browed and firm-nosed, with the expressive curve of lip and the blue, somehow tender eyes that move you so in a loyal, sensitive animal. But it was the purity in that face, scowl or smile, that struck you first. You realized that the emotions surfaced on it unimpeded. Mothers warmed to him immediately: they thought him nice, respectful, even shy. Girls inspected him, their gazes snagged by those bony, Breton good looks, that ingathered aura of dense, somehow *buried* maleness.

He was moody, there were always weathers in his soul. You would see the cloud pass over his sun; you would see the light go out of his face; he would become as dismal as November, and sit there with an odd *heaviness* about him, saying only the perfunctory least, ungiving, dour beyond help of a joke, as gloomy as an old New England house on a rainy afternoon. But, when it came, his smile was as dewy, radiant and optimistic as the first hour of sun on a May morning. He beamed with an irresistible belief in the equity of things, laughing at himself under his breath, playful, warm and giving off warmth, his mind flowing impetuously out of his mouth, his eyes flashing with humors: everything about him exuded his pleasure in you, simply because you were there.

Above all, he had that quality of charisma, presence, undivided flow of being, that is neither character nor charm, but something different, something more elusive and more rare: call it certainty, or daemon; call it a hint of the integrity of the soul that some people give off like an aroma. Lawrence had it, they say. Love him or hate him, he was always *there*—as a cataract is there, or a snake. Kerouac had it too. You always felt the strong pull of his special view of the world. The uniqueness of his ego was magnetic. He was as genuine as a handcrafted weathervane—one of a kind, continually veering in the wind. Such people can be as exhausting as they are fascinating, and this is not because they live at a different pitch, but because they *always* live at it. Still, this quality of *thereness* is hard to resist, and I responded to it in Kerouac as you respond to a recognition which you do not realize you have been awaiting until it comes. For I *had* been waiting, and was more dissatisfied with the attitudinizing of most of my other friends than I knew. I opened up to his exuberance without a moment's thought.

And meanwhile I read his novel alone one night in Alan Harrington's dim, lofty room on East 60th Street (mysteriously full of old newspapers), reaching into that yawning black bag for the succeeding notebooks, all of different sizes, and all filled to the margins with that angular, flowing rush of print that is his handwriting. I read on for hours, enthralled as only fiction, moving deeply and surely toward the achievement of its imagined world, can ever enthrall the reader. I was drawn down into the book, as you are drawn into a volume of Thackeray, or Dickens, or any of those huge, life-size novels of the nineteenth century that simply burst with innumerable, fascinating events—for *The Town and the City* was just such a crowded, essentially idealistic chronicle of many people living furiously, despite the sorrow that tinged its end.

Amazed by the energy of the book, I was also secretly relieved to discover (being an overly critical young man just then, unsure of his own creative gifts) that it wasn't really *contemporary* in the fashionable sense of that term—not soured, anxious, existential or Europeanized, and thus "posed no threat" to the bleakly allegorical novels the rest of us were trying to write. This foolishness was, of course, mainly a sop to my sophomoric preconceptions of the time, which, once thrown, freed me to the excitement that flowed out of the book like rainwater from a spout. Similarly conflicting reactions, on the part of people who should know better, still haunt most of the reviews of Kerouac's work with the unspoken complaint, "Why isn't he something other than he is?"

But more than the work, it was the man who attracted me. He was sympathetic, changeable, unsophisticated, quixotic, canny and madly imaginative. Whenever we were together, we always seemed to end up at dawn, on a street corner somewhere, still talking. He was at ease in all the myriad worlds outside my stuffy, bookish rooms, and was already absorbed in capturing, or being captured by, the vision of our generation that would become uniquely his. In little more than two months after our meeting, we were close enough friends for him to entrust his work journals to my eye.

I responded instinctively to the Kerouac I encountered there: the Kerouac who noted down each day's hoard of completed words, and then figured up his overall batting average; who zealously recorded his slumps along with his streaks, and just as zealously pep-talked or remonstrated with himself; the Kerouac, dizzied by the odors of the spring but chained in solitude by the mad endeavor that is the writing of a novel, who actually tried, with frustrated defiance, to *screw* the earth one night, to simply thumb a hole into the loam, and mate with it, so that he could get on with the task; the Kerouac who wanted to blow a lot of Spenglerian wind into the sails of a book that was already under full canvas on its own; who, in those doldrums of midpassage, those horse latitudes that one reaches in the second half of a long exhausting project, wondered pensively whether his book was "intellectually substantial," after all, but who, nevertheless, could write at the end:

> "Sept. 9. Tonight I finished and typed the last chapter. Last sentence of the novel: 'There were whoops and greetings and kisses and then everybody had supper in the kitchen.' Do you mean that the folks of this country won't like this last chapter?—or would it have been better if I had said, 'Everybody had dinner in the dining room . . .' But the work is finished."

In these journals, I saw the very work problems that were defeating me shouldered toward solutions; I saw my own confusion about the times spelled out, grappled with, forced to its crisis, and clarified in the act of fiction; and, above all, I saw a man, no more fortunate on the surface of it than myself, tirelessly clutching at his special truth—as any writer must.

When I had finished the last notebook, I felt an emotion unfamiliar enough in me to demand immediate expression, and longed to call him up (though he had no phone, just then, in Ozone Park), for I was filled with prideful idealism in our common craft; a keener sense of what must be given to it than I had ever had before; admiration for the stubborn, tender, lonesome, angry spirit that spoke from those pages; and something else I neither knew how to recognize nor handle: something almost familial, as if in this account of his consciousness my own had recognized a still-unexpressed fragment of itself; as if the impulsive reflex in him, and the wary reflex in me, were responses to an identical feeling about the world; as if he was an older, wilder brother, utterly unlike me, but sharing the same blood, shaped by the same life in the same house, and embodying the other half of a strong and ambivalent family trait. I wrote him a long, meandering letter, trying to tell him this, but lost the feeling in chagrin.

I mark that night as the start of the curious interaction between my nature and his. I mark it, as well, as the night when I began to be a writer in all seriousness. For something had been summoned out of me: I had glimpsed the potentials and the costs of the vocation; I had seen articulated what was still inchoate in my own mouth; I had taken a first step outwards by acknowledging (against my own timidities) that this man's view of the task was a view through which I might somehow come into my own best self as a writer.

In one of Kerouac's books, Duluoz writes to Cody that he is "haunted in the mind by you (think what that means, try it reverse, say, supposing you referred all your sensations to somebody and wondered what they thought . . . supposing each time you heard a delightfully original idea . . . you immediately slapped it over to check with the CODY THING." For some years, I did just this with Kerouac, checking my ideas, my perceptions, my emotions, and even my braver sentences, with the Kerouac, uncannily astute and inexhaustibly creative, who always looked over my shoulder in my imagination. Every young writer has a catalyst, and he was mine.

Later, his vision and his style would prove as contagious to others as they did to me during those apprentice years. Later, he would be parroted with a literalness that was anything but flattering. What *I* got from him, however, was not a voice, but an eye. "Reality is details," he would say, and you cut as close to the bone of the detail as words would go. A *decrepit* bureau was infinitely creakier, and emptier, and older than an *ancient* one. Rueful was sadness plus regret. Punctuation was the movie-music of prose. Form should be poetically satisfying, rather than mechanically demonstrable. And ultimately the writer's task was to write the book that he, himself, would most want to read, and to amass "a daily heap of words" toward that end. Beyond these rudiments, I tried to develop his instinct for the moment when gravity became pretension, and emotion turned to sentiment. "Always pull back," he would suggest, "and see how silly it all must look to God."

Once I gave him a chapter of which I was very proud at the time, an intensely Dostoyevskian confrontation between two overwrought young men, each of whom finally expresses a truth about himself which the other fails to notice. I was worried about the ending of this chapter because, no matter how I rewrote it, I couldn't seem to erase the tone of false solemnity that turned it ludicrous. Kerouac read the last paragraph several times—impatiently, almost indifferently—and then scribbled down the simple exclamation "Goodness me!" as the final comment by the weariest of the two. "That's what he'd say . . . See, now he retreats, he feels embarrassed, he sees how funny they are, talking like a couple of Raskolnikovs that way." It was precisely the right note, it restored the perspective in a flash, and this kind of warm canniness, this eye for the sad nonsense of life, has gone mostly unnoticed by Kerouac's critics (busily reacting to his material, as most of them are), but it is an essential part of his view, because his compassionate interest in humankind is grounded, at the bottom, in a fond awareness of its follies.

But if my writing was under his spell in those days (the four years difference in our ages put me four years behind him in experience and skill), my life was not. Though our New England backgrounds were somewhat similar, we were drawn in different directions. I was married, and rooted in New York. I was ambitious for fame and money, and had not yet come upon my own themes. Kerouac, on the other hand, was trying to find a fate to which he could consign himself. He was trying to make a soul-choice, for once and all, between the cozy nest of love and work the boy he had once been longed to build (particularly when in revulsion against cities, and city-centerlessness), and the wild road of freedom and possibility to which the man he was becoming was so powerfully attracted.

These were the years of his obsession with Neal Cassady (the "Cody" of the books); the Neal he had met a few years earlier, whose raw energies drew Kerouac back and forth across the continent time and time again; in whom he invested for a while all his deep, and deeply thwarted, fraternal emotions; and from whose vagabond joys and woes he created his most vivid portrait of the young, rootless American, high on life. For in the "Cody" books, Kerouac expresses most clearly his vision of America, "an Egyptian land" at once cruel and tender, petty and immense; and in "Cody" himself, he embodies both the promise of America's oldest dream (the unbuttoned soul venturing toward a reconciliation of its contradictions) and the bitter fact of its contemporary debauching (the obscenely blinking police car that questions anyone "moving independently of gasoline, power, Army or police"). As Americans always have, Kerouac hankered for the West, for western health and openness of spirit, for the immemorial dream of freedom, joy, communion and Oriental Oneness that even Concord-bound Thoreau always sauntered toward, and his peevish indictments of New York (and New Yorkishness) were symptomatic of his feeling that a certain reckless idealism, a special venturesomeness of heart, had been outlawed to the margins of American life in his time. His most persistent desire in those days was to chronicle what was happening on those margins.

But he was not always of one mind. Once, leaving my apartment with two Negro hipsters at dawn, off again across "all that," he glanced ruefully at my crowded bookshelves, my littered desk, the copy of *Doctor Faustus* I had been reading when he'd rung the bell hours before to say goodbye (all the conventional props of the author's room), and said with plaintive earnestness: "When I come back this time, I'm going to settle down for a while . . . . You know, and read everything again. Like this Thomas Mann, for instance . . . You'll see, John. That's just what I'll do." Then he went away, somehow reluctant to depart (I felt), as if he was already living ahead into all the sore-foot, dispiriting complications of penniless travel (for he never romanticized it, and always spoke of "the essential shame of hitchhiking"), half wondering, in the very moment of setting out, *why* in God's name he was doing it. But though he hesitated (and I always fancied that I saw the horror of being stranded in wintertime Butte in his eyes), he never turned away for long from the roaming, searching side of his nature, and the shifting tensions in his books result from the balancing of these ambivalences.

As a passionate believer in his talent, I felt that his ceaseless wandering was only putting off his "proper" work. I was always adjuring him to sit in one place long enough to write another *Town and City*; I lectured him about responsibility; I pelted him with letters detailing my vision of the books he should be writing. For a time, my surprising empathy for him deluded me into thinking that I knew him better than he knew himself, and I squirmed with querulous concern every time he came back from another harrowing jaunt to Mexico, his face haggard, his spirit somehow stretched taut, his feet unfeeling in his battered shoes—for all like a man staggering away from a debauch. I never fully understood the hunger that was gnawing in him then, and didn't realize the extent to which the breakup of his Lowell home, the chaos of the war years and the death of his father, had left him disrupted, anchorless; a deeply traditional nature thrown out of kilter, and thus enormously sensitive to anything uprooted, bereft, helpless or persevering: a nature intent on righting itself through the creative act. But though I was often mystified by the unfoldings in his work during those years, I knew that his temperament was entirely too obstinate, too unique, and too driven to be corralled by anyone. He simply had to dowse wherever his forked stick led him, no matter how parched the acre seemed. And somehow he always found a spring.

But that spring was in himself, not (as I thought) in the outside world he seemed intent on swallowing in a single, Gargantuan gulp; and tapping it was not (as most people still think to this day) simply a matter of sinking down a pipe and letting the water gush. When off the road in those days, he was mostly trying to write *On the Road*, finding, through all his successive attempts, that the traditional, "novelistic" form of *The Town and the City* was not fluid enough to contain the formlessness of the experience he was attempting to set down. "It's all an overlay," he kept insisting stubbornly. "It's added on afterwards. That isn't the truth . . . I want *deep* form, poetic form—the way the consciousness *really* digs everything that happens."

When he came by in the late afternoons, he usually had new scenes with him, but his characters never seemed to get very far beyond the many-layered New York milieu a well-made novel seemed to demand as a contrast to all the footloose uprootedness to come. He wrote long, intricate Melvillian sentences that unwound adroitly through a dense maze of clauses; astonishing sentences that were obsessed with simultaneously depicting the crumb on the plate, the plate on the table, the table in the house, and the house in the world, but which (to him) always got stalled in the traffic jam of their own rhetoric. To me, on the contrary, the writing was the acme of brilliance—cadenced, powerful, cresting toward an imminent beach, and I could never understand why it dissatisfied him so. I would have given anything I owned to have written such tidal prose, and yet he threw it out, and began again, and failed again, and grew moody and perplexed.

Then one day (he was married at the time, living in a large, pleasant room in Chelsea, doing book synopses for 20th-Century-Fox, and more remote from the road than I had ever known him), he announced irritably: "You know what I'm going to do? I'm going to get me a roll of shelf-paper, feed it into the typewriter, and just write it down as fast as I can, exactly like it happened, all in a rush, the hell with these phony architectures—and worry about it later."

Though anything I wrote off the top of my head was only fit to wipe shoes on, this method of composition sounded like good therapy at least, and when I visited him a few days after that, I heard his typewriter (as I came up the stairs) clattering away without pause, and watched, with some incredulity, as he unrolled the manuscript thirty feet beyond the machine in search of a choice passage. Two and a half weeks later, I read the finished book, which had become a scroll three inches thick made up of one single-spaced, unbroken paragraph 120 feet long, and knew immediately that it was the best thing he had done.

It was not another *Town and City*. The warmth, the hope, the youthful melancholy of that book had darkened, toughened, and matured. The eager chronicler of family suppers had become the fatalistic shambler after a carfull of horizon chasers, and the lyrical, Wolfean tone had grown as urgent and discordant as the times. Though I loved the book, though it awed me, though I felt as protective about it as if it had been my own (and later helped a little in getting it to sympathetic eyes), it disturbed me too, for in it I caught my first glimpse of the Kerouac to come, a Kerouac for whom I was oddly unprepared: a lonely, self-communing, mind-stormed man—still devout, though in a ruin of faiths; persistently celebrating whatever flower had managed to survive our bitter, urban weeds; indefatigable of eye, and fumy of mind; haunted by a reflex of love in the very pit of rude sensation; and, above all, hankering—hankering for an end: for truth to finally end the relativism, for harmony to somehow end the violence, so that peace would come to the young of this era, who were the heirs of both—and, failing that, for death. Something murmured behind the reckless onrush of the prose. It wasn't quite audible, but it accounted for the note of distant, fleeting sibilance that reverberated within the book's headlong syncopations. And for the first time, I suspected that underneath his youthful energy and jubilant thirst for life this man was immeasurably old in his soul.

It is difficult to articulate, but as the years have passed he has seemed more and more an old spirit to me; folk-old, poet-old, not of this world; like a ragged, tipsy old Li Po, thrashing around down there in the river marshes, muttering verses to himself by his fire of twigs in the dusk, allowing reality to pass through him unobstructed, writing messages back from solitude. Perhaps this is why his evocation of every gas tank, railyard, skidrow and streetcorner that he has ever seen is so hallucinatory, so charged with feeling, and yet so strangely muted by the perspective of our common destination. In any case, it has always struck me as curious that no one hears the old man's garrulity, nostalgia, sense-pleasure, stubbornness and resignation behind his work, because in a special corner of my mind he always appears as an old vagabond going West alone.

I think I first spied this inmost Kerouac in *On the Road*, but he did not come fully into view until that book failed to find a publisher, despite the lionizing, evenings at the opera, and good reviews that had greeted *Town and City,* and Kerouac's hopes for a quick career seemed to vanish (as surely as Dreiser's did when *Sister Carrie* was suppressed by the very house that printed it), and there was nothing left for him to do except consign himself, without a lifeline, to that "huge, complicated inland sea they call America," to sink into despondency, like Dreiser, or somehow swim.

Swim he did, though from the shore his efforts sometimes looked like the flailings that help to drown a drowning man. He took a deep plunge into the continent (and himself), a plunge that lasted almost five years, during which he regularly surfaced in San Francisco (for work on the railroad), Mexico City (for writing and kicks), and New York (for the quiet days and drowsing nights of home life with his mother). Stubbornly, he kept writing during this impoverished time. Ironically, he came into full and unique voice precisely during this half decade of anonymity. Paradoxically, it constituted the most fruitful period of his life—a period of explosive creativity (an average of two books every twelve months) that is perhaps unequalled in contemporary American literature, except by the four years during which Faulkner wrote *The Sound and the Fury, As I Lay Dying, Sanctuary* and *Light in August.*

I saw less of him during those years, but his letters were absorbed in the struggle to throw his net wide enough to snare the feverish vision of his own life that was maturing in his imagination: "When I get to be so pure you won't be able to bear the thought of my death on a starry night (right now I've nothing to do with stars, I've lied so far) it will be when I'll have come to know and tell the truth (all of it, in every conceivable mask) and yet digress from that to my lyric-alto knowing of this land . . . a deep-form bringing together of two ultimate and at-present conflicting streaks in me." (July 14, 1951)

This feeling that he had "lied so far" had driven him to write *On the Road* as he did; rejection of the book by the publishers made it seem that there was no one to write for but himself, and little sense in writing "novels" that were not wanted anyway; and so he proceeded to dismantle all his hard-learned "artistries," seeking to free the whole range of his consciousness to the page—the consciousness that was one continuous, vivid flow of sense-data, associations, memories and meditations—until by the spring of 1952, he could write to me exultantly: "What I'm beginning to discover now is something beyond the novel and beyond the arbitrary confines of the story . . . into realms of revealed Picture . . .

wild form, man, wild form. Wild form's the only form holds what I have to say—my mind is exploding to say something about every image and every memory . . . I have an irrational lust to set down everything I know . . . at this time in my life I'm making myself sick to find the wild form that can grow with my wild heart . . . because now I KNOW MY HEART DOES GROW . . ." Though I didn't always comprehend what he was driving at, I always encouraged him (as did all his friends), because there was simply no distrusting a man who burned as purely as he was burning then.

The letters kept arriving—tortured, angry, pensive, triumphant, bitter with complaints, insistently creative; letters from west coast Mexico, from L.A. slums, from rusty tankers and Washington state lumber towns; letters that traced (for me) the progress of a man gradually sinking out of sight, down into the darks of life and Self, below "literature," beyond the range of its timid firelight. Manuscripts kept arriving too, sent haphazardly across thousands of miles of road, wrapped in brown paper bags, unregistered, uninsured, often with no carbon copy at the other end in case of loss.

I read them eagerly. I read each one at a single sitting. And I always had the same reaction. I was overcome each time by a strange mixture of exhilaration and depression. Some linchpin had been pulled in those books, some floodgate had been opened, and Kerouac wrote like a man unhinged by his own prescience, as helpless as someone under LSD to control the movement of his consciousness backwards and forwards over his life. I imagined him (a lightning typist since his youth) sitting at the machine, staring into the blankness of the space in front of him, careful not to *will* anything, and simply recording the "movie" unreeling in his mind. Somehow the words were no longer words, but had become things. Somehow an open circuit of feeling had been established between his awareness and its object of the moment, and the result was as startling as being trapped in another man's eyes.

For me, reading those books was like recklessly diving through a surf you have underestimated. At first, the green shimmer of the subterranean world beneath the waves intoxicates you with the daring of your own species; then all at once the power and the reality of the element in which you are trespassing comes home to you, and for one moment the danger and the joy are so absolutely intermingled that something in you shrinks back from going deeper, from knowing more. I shrank back from Kerouac's books. I feared for his mind out there, and sometimes for my own. His eye was like a fine membrane vibrating between the intolerable pressure of two walls of water: the consciousness flowing outward to absorb everything in the drench of thought; and reality flooding inward to drown everything but the language to describe it. My eerie sense of kinship with him gave his work a reality for me that always seemed to overwhelm my own life for a while.

This curious reaction was intensified by my hope that he would write something that would earn him a settled life. But every new book he sent me seemed to beat more obstinately against the literary currents of the time, and I found myself in a paradox that was distinctly uncomfortable for a serious man: so passionately did I long for his work to be given the recognition it deserved, that sometimes I caught myself wishing he would blunt the edge of it a little toward that end. Also, I must confess, I did not always have the courage of my own tastes. I remember, for instance, reading *Visions of Cody* one muggy afternoon, and then going out to walk by the East River, cursing Kerouac in my head for writing so well in a book which, I was firmly convinced, would never be published. To this day, whenever I grow complacent about my own good sense, I recall that river walk. I recall that I cursed him, rather than the publishers, or the critics, or the culture itself that was excluding him. Some years later, I reread *Cody* with a feeling of amazement at my own confusion that was fully as great as my shame, for it was immediately apparent that it contained prose of an eloquence that was Elizabethan, in an accent that was indelibly that of our postwar generation.

Notoriety came suddenly in 1957, and with it money, adulation, TV appearances, interviews, scandals, and another sort of crucible (the crucible of the public eye) than any Kerouac had survived already. That notoriety was mostly based on *On the Road*, a book six years old, written by a man he was only second cousin to any longer, and yet people invariably looked at him, spoke to him, and deferred to him, as if he *was* that other man, for the Beat Generation was news by then, and Kerouac (they thought) *was* the Beat Generation.

They tended to drive their cars more recklessly when he was with them, as if he was "Dean Moriarty," and not the Kerouac who hated to drive and whom I had once seen crouching on the floor of a car, in a panic, during a drunken, six-hour dash from New York to Provincetown. They plied him with drinks, they created parties around him, they doubled the disorder in the hopes of catching his eye, and so never glimpsed the Kerouac who once confessed to me: "You know what I'm thinking when I'm in the midst of all *that*—the uproar, the boozing, the wildness? I'm always thinking: What am I doing here? Is this the way that I'm *supposed* to feel?" They peeked at him as if he was some Petronius Arbiter of cool, detached hipness, and saw, to their confusion, a man who always turned the volume up, who tapped his feet and exulted, and loathed the hostility for which coolness was a mask. They saw the seeker after continuity who, no matter how rootless his life may seem, has always known that our anguish is uprootedness. Wherever he went, he was confronted by that other man. Once in L.A., alone in a coffee house, he tried to strike up a conversation with the guy behind the counter, saying, "Hey, I'm Jack Kerouac. Let's have a talk or something," to which the guy replied with hip disdain: "Sure you are. They all say that." A few such encounters produce the bizarre feeling that one is invisible, and there were many such.

On top of this, he heard his writing praised as "rollicking" or damned as "typing," knowing that both opinions were probably based on a reading of no more than *On the Road*—in some ways his most carelessly written book. *Doctor Sax, Cody, Tristessa, Lonesome Traveler*—all the books in which his voice is most assured and his vision clearest—were either dismissed or ignored, because they did not easily jibe with the image of the adolescent, kicks-hungry yawper that has dogged Kerouac's career as relentlessly as the image of the South Sea Island tale-teller dogged Melville's. He saw the Buddhist reverence for all sentient life, which months alone on mountaintops and years in the glut of cities had only reinforced in him, repeatedly labelled "gibberish" and "nonsense" by men who relegated "reverence," without a qualm, to the religion shelves of their libraries, and then called him uneducated. And the man who wrote me fifteen years ago, "Life is drenched in spirit; it rains spirit; we would *suffer* were it not so" (and believes it still), lived to see the books which embodied this credo on page after page used as bibles of hipness by the Beatniks, derided as incoherent mouthings by the critics, and treated as some kind of literary equivalent of rock'n'roll by the mass media.

The years went by; the books appeared one by one; he moved ceaselessly back and forth between Long Island and Florida; and he went on writing just the same.

In 1960, it became a mystery to me why he did it: he seemed to care less and less about things like "career" and "reputation." All of a sudden, I couldn't understand any longer what made him continue. I remembered Melville (the American writer Kerouac most resembles in temperament); I remembered that something had abandoned Melville in midlife—some unexamined faith, some fruitful illusion, which had cohered in him long enough for the early novels to get written. I remembered, as well, that Hawthorne, sensing its absence in 1856, had sadly reported that Melville had "pretty much made up his mind to be annihilated." And suddenly I felt, with a shiver, that Kerouac would not live much beyond forty. Such voracious appetites, such psychic vulnerability, such singleness of purpose, must (I felt) ream a man out at the end, and the Kerouac I knew was as incapable of turning away from his own consuming consciousness, as he was of living for long once he had been burned out by it. Still (I told myself), eight years after Hawthorne's insight, he himself was dead of the very abandonment he had felt in the other man, while Melville, living on into that quiet obscurity that comes to men who have *passed through* themselves, turned as naturally to poetry as aging men turn to gardening. Perhaps with Kerouac it would be the same.

Whenever we got together, however, I was not so sure. We always seemed to sit and drink—sometimes for a week. In the beginning, we would talk and talk and talk, but then we would grow strangely silent, as if there was no more need to say certain things. During these silences, I caught myself looking at Kerouac, as you look at all tremendously gifted, tremendously complicated men, wondering where in God's name the damned vision comes from.

I saw a man, often quarrelsome, sometimes prone to silly class resentments, as defensive as a coyote on the scent, and as intractable as a horse that will not take a saddle; a man who sometimes seemed positively crazed by the upheavals in his own psyche, whose life was painfully wrenched between the desire to know, for once and all, just *who* he was, and the equally powerful desire to become immolated in a Reality beyond himself. I saw a man who (for as long as I had known him) had undeviatingly pursued his vision of the dislocations and attritions of his generation's experience "in great America," undeterred by failure or despair, so selflessly enlisted in its service that the man and the vision were inseparable; the process by which one fed the other (and vice versa) too organic and too mysterious to comprehend, and the only word inclusive enough to contain the full range of all the gifts, and all the flaws, that vague word, "genius." Looking at Kerouac, I realized he was the single writer I had ever known for whom no other word would do. And yet I could not shake off the premonition that he would vanish suddenly.

Then one day an odd thing happened. A few miles up a bad stretch of road, imperilled by an autumn flood, a few years ago, I drove into Marquette, Iowa, under the bleak Mississippi palisades, in a dismal rain, and there, at the end of the street, saw Burke's Hotel—grimy, plain as coffee grounds, soot-enlayered, in need of paint, redolent of iron bedsteads, damp sheets, forlorn unopened

Gideons, smoke-blackened paneling in the shadowy lobby, and corrugated tin ceilings of 1930s cobwebs. There it was, *decrepit* as a bureau under the forbidding, wild escarpment in the river drizzle, with its steamy lunchroom full of greasy smells, and its barbershop of rusty fans: an end-of-the-road hotel, marooned in that rainy Saturday afternoon, in that town of a few woeful beer taverns and hardware stores—the huge bluffs of the awesome river looming over it.

Instantly, I thought of Kerouac, for the place was quintessentially *his* America, the America he knows down to its last stained mattress ticking and its final broken bottle in the railroad weeds; the America he taught me how to see, full of the anxious faces in which his eye has spied an older, more rooted America (of spittoons, and guffawing, and winter suppers), now vanishing bewilderedly behind the billboards and TV antennas; an America whose youths stand around on the street corners, undecided, caught in the discrepancy between the wild longings they feel and the tame life they get; a land (now in its sour time) which Kerouac goes on evoking in the accents most native to it: "I loved the blue dawns over racetracks and made a bet Ioway was sweet like its name, my heart went out to lonely sounds in the misty springtime night of wild sweet America in her powers, the wetness of the wire fence bugled me to belief. I stood on sandpiles with an open soul." (There's all our uprootedness in that, and all our hungering for roots—what another American writer called our "complex fate": even truer of us now, in a century severed from its faiths.)

The special Kerouac mood was on that town, and, as I waited for the stoplight, realizing again how eloquently he has spoken for the pang of being young in America in this time, I imagined him there in Burke's Hotel, having a coffee behind the blurred plate glass, baseball-hatted and crepesoled for the road, weary and intent, something spectral and unnoticed about him down the counter there as the waitress gossiped—passing through, years ago, toward the promise of another coast.

I caught myself thinking: he has given this way of seeing to all of us. Then I missed him keenly, and knew for sure he would survive.

Novelist friends: Alan Harrington, Jack Kerouac, and John Clellon Holmes, early-1960s. Photo by Shirley Holmes.

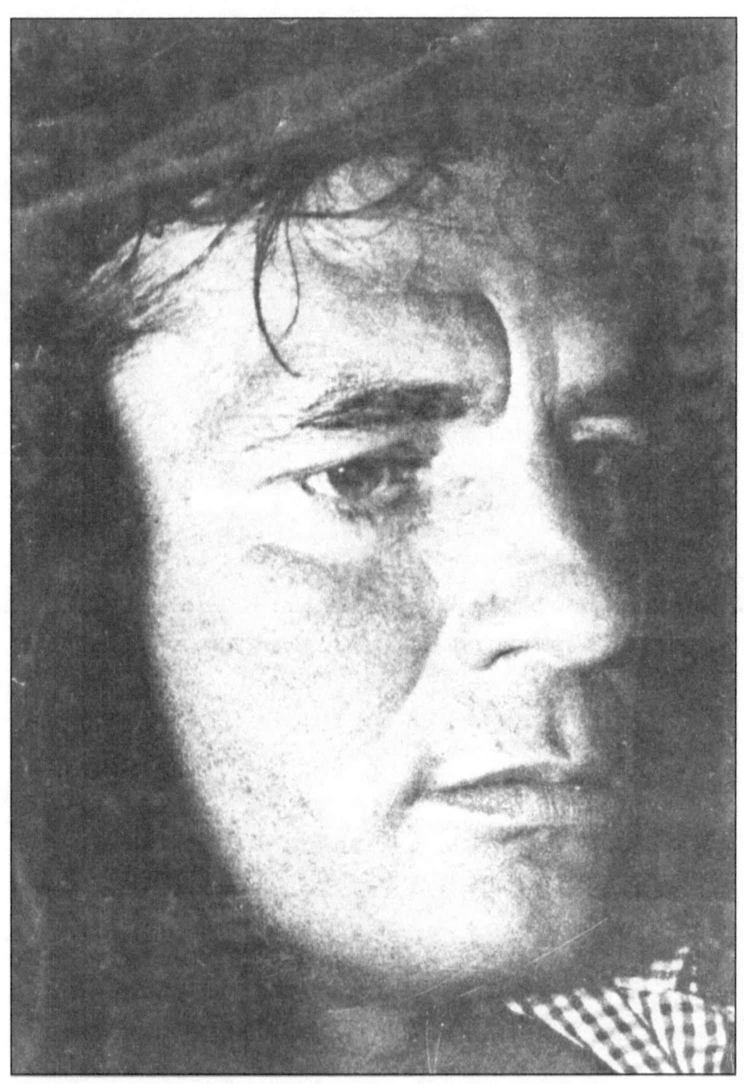

Jack Kerouac: Book jacket photo from Desolation Angels *(1965) and* Satori in Paris *(1966) by Lawrence L. Smith.*

GONE IN OCTOBER

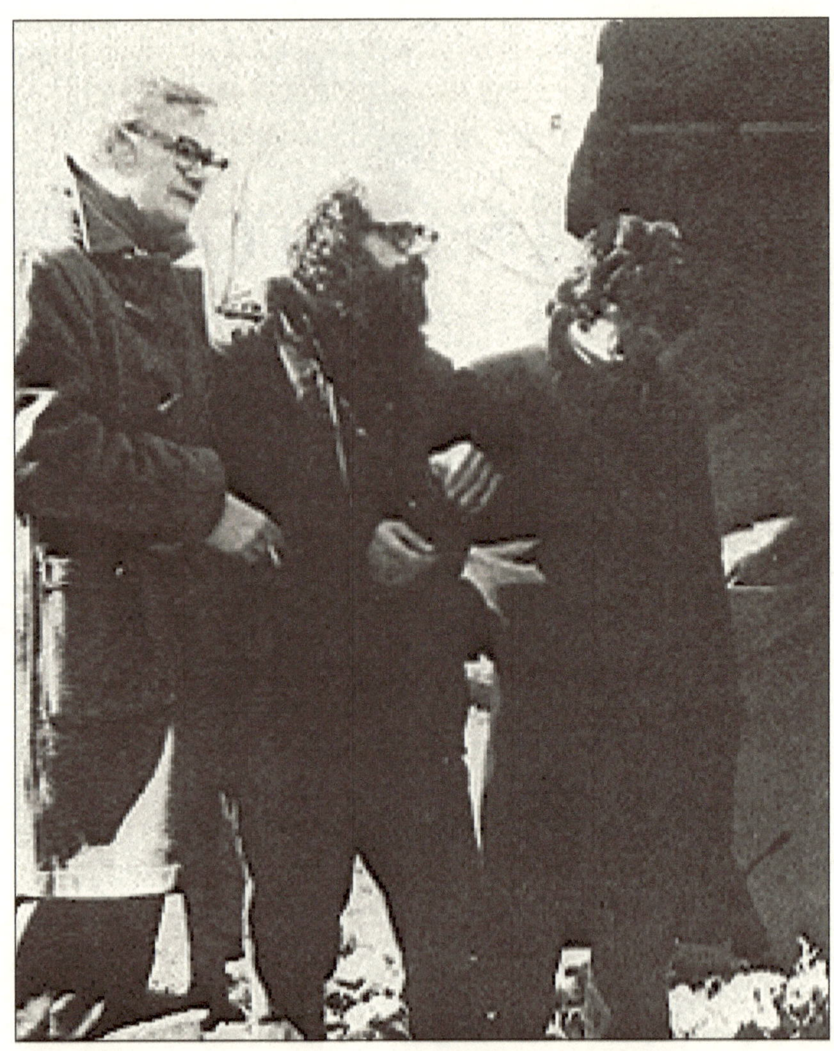

John Clellon Holmes, Allen Ginsberg, and Gregory Corso at Jack's grave, Lowell, Massachusetts, October 24, 1969. Photo by Ann Charters.

Journal: Oct. 21, 1969, 12:45 PM—Old Saybrook

Jack is dead in St. Pete. I was reading about him in an old journal when Shirley called out from downstairs, having heard it on the radio. There were the bad, pointless moments waiting for a repeat of the newscast; there were the waves of awareness coming up and then receding . . . . I have always addressed my sentences to him, to his disapproving canny eye, and it will be different to write from now on . . . Allen G. called. By happenstance, he will be in New Haven tomorrow, and we will go down. "He didn't live much beyond Neal," Allen said as a matter of interest. "Only a year and a half" . . . I spoke to Gregory & Peter too—they were all at the Cherry Valley farm . . . We wired Memère & Stella hopeless, useless words. Portents of his death somewhere, sometime, have plagued me for 8-10 years—as recently as last Thursday I thought of him dying in St. Louis or Chicago on some Kerouac-crazy trip . . . I haven't dared think of his mind in its last hours. What can one say? He's gone. It's over for him.

ONE

SHIRLEY AND I DROVE DOWN TO NEW HAVEN for Ginsberg's reading at Yale under clear high skies of blue. The trees had turned in the last days to full autumn, and the afternoon before (walking the fact into consciousness), I'd thought that it was apt that Jack had gone away in October, which was his favorite month, and that now it was one of those red and gold New England afternoons through which footballs used to loft in such brave arcs when we were young.

No more Jack, I repeated to myself as I drove, his death a fact too inexplicable, too final, to go down. I'd known him for half my life. Whatever sort of man and writer I'd become was due in no small measure to our friendship. As young men, we had shared those important, exuberant years that sometimes shape the rest of life. *Damn him!* I caught myself thinking. *Why does he do things like this?* I'd talked to him for an hour on the phone not ten days ago, and we had bickered as we often did when he was drunk, and he had challenged me to call him back in an hour, and I hadn't done it, exasperated by his boozy monologs. And now the phone was permanently dead.

We parked near the Yale Co-Op, and walked through chilly streets to the Political Union Library where the students were holding a reception for Allen. In a paneled, upstairs room, twenty or thirty young people, drinking port and sherry, sat on the floor around the ringleted, Karl Marx beard spread out benignly on Allen's chest, and his dome of balding forehead gave him the look of a worldly Talmud scholar who had retired to the Negev. Gregory squatted on his heels in an enormous, George Raft overcoat, working on a tumbler of sherry, and Peter, now become a grizzled wrangler of bitter winters in upstate New York, stared silently out from under the three-inch brim of a hat of day-glo red. It was the first time that we had all been in the same room in over five years.

In the middle of a long answer about ecology, Allen waved, and Gregory came over, whispering, "What a time to get together, huh?"

Allen finished, and he and Peter worked their way through the crowd of students, and we embraced. "I hardly recognized you in your tweedy-professor disguise," Allen said, though actually I had on a red flannel shirt and a corduroy suit. "Well, old Jack's dead, I guess," he added, and we looked at one another, wordless with the fact.

"Yup."

We straggled through the evening streets towards dinner with some of the students, arranging that the three of them would drive home with us that night, and we'd all go up to Lowell the next day for the funeral. Then on to the reading, which was held in a large, dingy, high-ceilinged hall, already filled with young people in their army jackets, beards, ragged blue jeans, maidenly falls of hair, love beads and peace amulets—the army of the war against the death-drive in the modern world, which, for some of us, had already been going on for two decades. We were taken down front to wait, and there on the stage was a paper banner, twelve by four feet in size, on which was written: "IN MEMORIAM: Jack Kerouac, 1922-1969," and below that: "Neal Cassady, 1927-1968."

Allen and Peter came down the side aisle, and up onto the stage with their harmonium, where they removed their jackets to get down to work. Gregory, who was down in the audience with us, filmed all this with an expensive, zoom-lensed movie camera and glistening tripod (he was into film now; he filmed bits and pieces of everything; he was making a record of his existence). Allen introduced us all from the stage, and the reading started. "We'll begin with a prayer," he said, and he and Peter began chanting a Sutra, Jack's Sutra, the Diamond, standing together in their shirts, Peter palming the bellows of the harmonium with the metronomic motion of a weaver with his beater, and both wailing the clear, high-pitched chant, which was followed by a scatter of applause from the perplexed, politicalized students, who expected something more inflammatory, or more "relevant." Allen was quietly remonstrative. "You don't have to applaud a prayer," he said.

Then he read three or four choruses from Jack's *Mexico City Blues,* repeating the *211th Chorus*, "The wheel of the quivering meat conception," because of the lines:

> "*Poor*! I wish I was free
> of that slaving meat wheel
> and safe in heaven dead"

He repeated this three times for emphasis, as if to say: 'See, there's your politics, that's your art, that's your reality, *that* was life to him.' Then he read the last *Chorus* with some deliberation:

"Vanish.
Which will be your best reward,
T'were better to get rid
John O'Twill, then sit a-mortying
In this Half Eternity with nobody
To save the old man being hanged
In my closet for nothing
And everybody watches
When the act is done—
Stop the murder & the suicide!
All's well!
I am the Guard"

Perhaps no one on the outside of Jack's life ever really understood these lines, but years ago they had made me realize he didn't want to stay in such a world, and even say as much in *Nothing More to Declare,* and have him chide me about putting him in his grave. After this, Allen read for almost an hour out of his own poems, mostly from *Planet News*, the ones addressed to Jack, those couched as questions, particularly one entitled, *Why is God love, Jack?*, with its stubborn celebratory end:

"Seeking still seeking the
thrill-delicious
bliss in the
heart abdomen loins
& thighs
Not refusing this
38 yr. 145 lb. head
arms & feet of meat
Nor one single Whitmanic
toenail condemn
nor hair prophetic banish
to remorseless Hell,
Because wrapped with machinery
I confess my ashamed desire."

The kids were now a little less confused, they had been absorbed into the poetry by Allen's quiet austerity and were having a *political* experience after all, and Allen went on, losing some, making no comment, but working on the remnant, knowing what he was about.

Then he said: "I've been setting some of Blake's poems to music, and Peter and I will sing a few after we take ten minutes off, so John Holmes can hear them," and after the break they both turned to look down at me, Allen smiling with the healing euphoria of song, having been able to add something at last to our old master, Blake—if it was only these incantatory, Hebraic, sing-song melodies that piped so wild.

When they were done, Allen opened it up to questions from the audience, and the questions weren't too silly, just a little solemn with the "non-negotiable" puritanism of kids that year, who seemed so hungry for confrontation that it suggested a psychic rather than a political need, and who often didn't seem to realize that all radical politics are a response to a spiritual crisis—or, as Ginsberg believes, it's all your own Being. You're not separate from the process you wish to change, much less from the older processes of Nature. It's all of us—aphids, Nixon, buffalos, Dylan—all together in the ecological twilight.

Then a blond kid got up, somewhat shy, be-spectacled, grave and confused, and stumbled out that he thought they'd like to know what Allen thought about Kerouac's death, and where Jack fit into the scene today, and why he seemed to have drifted off into curious cranky ideas in recent years, and should they care about him. Was he—well, *important*? They couldn't say. Would Allen?

Allen sighed and leaned on the lectern towards the microphone on his elbows, and didn't say anything for fifty seconds. I knew what he was thinking: How could you sum it up in a few glib words? How could you bring back the eager Jack, Jack of the tender eyes, the raucous Jack of midnights, Jack's earnest sweat, maddening Jack of the end of the nights, maudlin Jack of all the songs, the Jack who knew for sure, canny Jack who trusted to his whims, Jack simple as a cornflower, fist-proud Jack, the bongo-Jack of saucepans, Jack of the Chinese restaurants, Jack mooning under streetlamps about guilt, the Jack of Jacks?—when all they probably knew anything about was drunken, contentious Jack, bigoted, mind-stormed Jack, the Jack of sneers, the boozy bum of Buckley, the imitator of Stepin Fetchits who wrote all those unreadable books, and somehow now appeared to have drunk a hole in his Balzac-belly. How could you? No way.

But Allen gathered his thoughts, and leaned closer to the mike, and simply said: "Well, he was the first one to make a new crack in the consciousness," and everything else—pot, Rock, doin' your thing, make a new Jerusalem, etc., had come out of that crack. "Years ago, he rolled around on my floor, laughing his head off at something I'd said, and said, 'Allen, you're a hairy loss,' and I concluded he was only drunk again, but then, of course, I am, that's what I am. I admitted it a few years ago. And you see, he knew that—like he knew that he was only a lonesome, self-absorbed Canuck, a big dumb Dharma bum." And what he had done was to try to follow the implications of this sad-comic view of things down to the bottom of his own nature, and transcribe it in its own on-rushing spontaneous flow, and leave it there for later, for others.

"So he drank himself to death," Allen said bluntly, "which is only another way of living, of handling the pain and foolishness of knowing that it's all a dream, a great, baffling, silly emptiness, after all." And then abruptly he said nothing more.

There were a few more questions, and then he read *Wales Visitation* (his ecology-revelation of 1967, in which the simple one-ness of all organic life had come home to him on Acid), after which he and Peter did *Hare Krishna* for an end, and lo-and-behold most of these politicalized kids joined in—the girls swaying to the chant and staring pensively inward, the young solemn faces of the boys washed of schismatic bad trips for that moment, everyone chanting softly, abashedly in that large, echoing auditorium, everyone standing up towards the finish, and then drifting away when it was over. We milled around waiting for Allen to get free of those special few who always pass you notes after an appearance, notes that read: The Age of Aquarius is here, I am into realms of light, come and use me for anything. Or: If you are ever near Santa Fe, look up So-and-so, she's So-and-so's cousin, and she's one of us. Or: Could I send you my poem that I wrote coming off Speed on Saturday, Oct. 10, 1968, when I discovered that I am a flea in God's whisker?

Allen had to go tape an interview for the university radio station, so Gregory and Shirley and I went to clean out the dormitory room they had been assigned but wouldn't need now. As we hurried through the bitter cold New Haven streets, struggling with the heavy camera and tripod, Gregory said: "They always keep you talking that way, like they never had anyone they could *really* talk to, but I say to them, 'Listen, I was born when people smoked straights and drank booze. Let me have a drink and I'll noodle your doodle, or save your soul—whatever you're after—'," laughing in a breathless, delighted little cackle, which, the next day, driving to Lowell, I would hear from the backseat—heh-heh-heh-heh-heh-heh—and realize, "By God, it's Jack's laugh, Gregory laughs like Jack now, modestly, as at some private thought, *happy.*" I'd forgotten Jack's old laugh, he hadn't laughed that way much in recent years, not that soft *heh-heh-heh* of pleasure, and I remembered it without a pang.

We went through shadowy quads as icy as your winter nose-tip, shrouded students hurrying home under old elms, and up into the dorm to collect their stuff: Gregory's camera case, a suitcase of what Jack used to call "needments," a green sports shirt and a pair of jockey shorts drying on the Venetian blind. Shirley made us a bourbon in the single-tooth glass, and we sipped it while Gregory told us about how they had gone out into the upstate woods after they heard the news about Jack, just the day before, all of them up in Cherry Valley, and carved Jack's initials into a tree—"You know, in the name of American poetry."

We struggled all the baggage down into my car, and then walked down the block to the radio station where Allen sat in a smokebleared recording-booth with seven or eight student-activists, patiently going into his sixth straight hour of talk. Gregory and I went in for a minute, to be interviewed too, but of course the three of us kept drifting into personal things, having had no real chance till then—such as how the rain-water runs down the stone embankments in Eureka Springs, Arkansas, and how, yes, we'd all been there, though never together, and it was where Carry Nation conducted her last campaign against drink. The young men seemed bewildered by this, and one of them finally said: "Why do you guys always talk about where people are from, and what happened there? Does all that really matter?" How explain?

It was too hot in the booth, and Shirley and Gregory and I went into another room, and waited, and finally Allen got free, and we piled into the car, and circled the large, deserted green with its row of ghostly churches, and got onto the Connecticut Turnpike, and talked about Jack at last: "Isn't it weird?" Allen kept saying. "What are we all doing here? Do you know why he drank like that, John? I don't understand *that* kind of drinking . . . But what did we do wrong? Do you think we should have made a greater effort to get down to Florida? Could we have *done* anything?"

I didn't think so. There was nothing one friend could do for another but accept his nature wholeheartedly, and in the last months, during those endless phone calls at unlikely hours that had become a habit with Jack, I had heard the booze speaking out of him like the voice of one of those baleful spirits that take possession of the soul in Gothic novels. But we had been far too close for the admonishments that are possible in shallower relationships. I knew he was serious, even about his dissipations, and the basic seriousness of a man's struggle with his destiny is beyond "help."

We drove the thirty-five miles home to Saybrook in the dark and cold, stars pin-bright like so many stars on so many driving-nights when we had all gone somewhere for forgotten reasons, full of expectations when we climbed into the car, only to become quenched and ruminant as the hours went by in the huge, graphic winter-night. Home to a fire, an immense bowl of Shirley's vegetable soup for famished Allen (who'd quit smoking), and whiskey for the rest of us.

Gregory had a bad toothache, and Peter kept scolding him for being chary of the dentist. "You'll have to go through life in your gums," he said—Peter who now ran the farm, planted gardens, milked cows, drove tractors, cooked, said they ought to sell that spavined horse "who just stands around"; and Peter who, the next morning, went all over our old house asking questions about how I'd raised "that beam there," was it hard cutting the fireplace opening, laying the hearth, getting it to draw? How much were our heat bills? Did our okra come up this year? How did we keep vegetables through the winter? The practical, rural Peter with his repeated, "Uh-*huh*," at everything anyone said, which meant: Yes, yes, okay, I get that, go on, uh-*huh*.

We all went off to bed eventually, all of us dead out, Allen saying as he glanced around my shelves: "Well, you have all Jack's books, I see. I kept lending mine away and I haven't got them anymore. Now I'll have to sit down and read them again, I guess,"—a funny, private little laugh admitting the ambiguities of the emotions at such a moment. Bone-tired, smoked-out, I had one more booze, but began to think, so didn't finish it, and slept the sleep of a hoarder-of-resources.

TWO

Up to the russets and ochres of an October day through which leaves scattered into bright drifts, a day that was bland in the sun but hinted at winter once you stepped out of it. I went off to get the car's broken heater fixed, which proved impossible on such short notice, but I got extra anti-freeze anyway in case we had a sudden drop of temperature overnight. When I got back, we all sat around, while Shirley made bisquits and fresh coffee, and ranged far afield in our separate intelligences.

At some remark of Gregory's, Allen launched into a description of the Gnostic theory of the universe. The basic idea (he explained) was that the Creation was only the first instant of the Void's awareness of itself, from which original act of consciousness all successive enlayerings of consciousness had come, each covering up the insight of the other, but all seeking to hide the knowledge of the perfect emptiness of origins (the snake-in-the-garden itself sent to tip us off to this truth), and from that, of course, the Western idea of evil had inevitably come.

"And you see, Jack knew all that," Allen said. "That's what he was writing about—the agony of differentiated consciousness. He knew it was all a dream."

"Still, he was stuck in it," Gregory said, "just like all of us."

It didn't seem unusual to be establishing a metaphysical ground from which to think about Jack's death. Simple sorrow for the friend was a private matter, an individual loss, but what he had been trying to say, the world of his unique eye, the still point towards which all the words were aimed, seemed necessary to know with some clarity that crisp October morning when at last we would all go to Lowell together. At one time or another, each of us had talked with Jack about doing it, and made impromptu plans, only to lose them in a fume of booze or distraction, and only Allen had ever made it for a night or two a few years before.

Over the coffee and bisquits, my mother arrived with maps to show me a quick route to Maine that would take us right by Lowell, and Allen put his arm around her in simple creaturely friendliness as she drew it out, though they hadn't seen one another in fourteen years, and then we all sat down for a while and talked—organic gardening, root-cellars, Scott Nearing, the properties of *bancha* tea. Gregory wanted to take movies of us all, and so we went out in front of the house in the cold sun, and lined up like members of *The Band*, Allen saying of my mother, "Behold, the survivor!" at which her eyes moistened, because she had known Jack for a long time, and, like most mothers, thought of him as a gifted and unruly man, in whom she glimpsed the loyal and affectionate son.

But it was time to go, and we took off up the Connecticut Turnpike through rolling hills, as richly mottled with autumn foliage as the texture of a parti-colored sponge, the car's rear-end slewing around with all the added weight, and the wind coming so strong across the highway that my wrists ached holding the car on the road. After a while, Allen and Peter got out the harmonium and sang for an hour, Allen saying: "What would you like to hear next? *London*? Yes, we've done that," and they performed it. "All right, what's next? Call out your favorites . . . No, I'm leaving *Tyger, Tyger* to the last because it's the most obvious and the hardest to do . . ."

The car rocked with wind and wailing voices as we rolled through little towns like Oxford, the birthplace of Clara Barton (It makes you remember it, kids. It marks it indelibly in your head. You think of her *there*), and Webster full of crazy, every-man-for-himself Massachusetts drivers, imperiling our carload of poets. I thought it might take us three and a quarter hours to get to Lowell, and as we neared the cutoff, roaring up Route 495 among the barrelling trucks, the day gloomed over (as I knew it would, as it had to near the "Snake Mountain" of *Doctor Sax*), the harsh, grey sky darkening with that hint of arctic north that always murmurs the mysterious word "Saskatchewan" to me—with its images of fir-forests awesome in winter—snow at twilight, and prairie immensities north of Dakota over the line, and finally the terrible majesties of the Canadian Rockies that make the mind ache with awareness of its own insignificance. In my time, only Jack had found a prose commensurate to the dimensions of the continent as they weighed on human consciousness. Most writers no longer even *tried* for that kind of range anymore.

Lowell, of course, turned out to be an ugly, ratchety mill town in unplanned sprawl along the Merrimack: shuttered factories, railyards blown with hapless papers, unpainted wooden buildings with their date-plaques blurred by weather over the doors, and the turreted Town Hall with the library next to it where Jack had read his Balzac when he was a polite, bow-tied, moody youth, when he was *Jackie* (as he was still Jackie to everyone who'd known him in Lowell)—all in a mad tangle of evening traffic on crazy, unmarked, one-way streets of cobble, all of it plain with that New England milltown brick-and-siding plainness.

My direction-signals weren't working properly, the nerves of driving in the rush of cars hurrying home to supper were wearing me down, but we got parked near where Allen thought Nick Sampas (Jack's brother-in-law) had a bar. We'd go in there and get located. We tumbled out into a bone-cold little square, all but grassless, the air full of those vagrant swirls of snowflakes that always seem to blow so forlornly in squares in the run-down part of any town where the drunks wander with chapped hands in old overcoats, and the Ballantine-signs in the saloons are the only coziness. We went into a bar that resembled Allen's recollection of Nick's place. Here we came—every honest Greek workingman's idea of what was wrong with the fucking country: long hair, beards, old coats, red hats, cracked shoes. And what was a pretty woman, in her black leather coat and black pumps, doing with a bunch of weirdos?

But, though we were strange to the drinkers there, they didn't freeze us with hostility, and Shirley and I had whiskies, while the others sipped a glass of wine apiece. It wasn't the right bar, after all, but the men in there knew the place we wanted: "Sure, Nicky's place, used to be the old Sixty-Six Club, cross town, you go up here, take your first right at the light, blah, blah, blah—," but they were helpful, and scrawled out the directions on a beer-coaster for Allen, who (used to being *everyone's* "hairy loss") quietly and politely persisted through the blunt stares of men to whom he must have seemed as alien as St. Francis in the Vatican.

Back to the car again. Peter took over the driving, and we went up to the first right, made the correct turn this time, went down further dreary blocks, and yes, there was Nick's—we'd come right by it on our way into the center of town. Beyond its steamy plate-glass, it was blissfully overwarm (the way I remembered small-town stores off New Hampshire winter sidewalks in the Thirties) and "modernized"—creamy, indirect lights set into the backbar, captain's-backed stools, a shuffleboard game, and a few tables in the eating-half of the place where you imagined rows of men dancing slow, arms-on-shoulders bouzouki-dances on Saturday nights.

Yes, the bartender said, he had that day's Lowell papers with the funeral plans, and, yes, he recognized Allen from the time Allen had been in there drinking with Jack some years ago, and, yes, Nick would be back anytime now. He'd gone out to Logan Airport to pick up Stella (Jack's wife) and Tony (another Sampas brother) who was bringing her up from St. Petersburg, but he'd be there shortly, and Jack's body was already in Lowell, having come in on an earlier flight. What did we want to drink?

We read the funeral announcement in the *Lowell Sun*: the body would be on view from seven to ten that night, the funeral was tomorrow morning at eleven at St. Jean Baptiste Cathedral. Allen seemed strangely sobered as we read this together: "It's such good, succinct prose," he said, "don't you think? . . . Hey, can I keep this?" to the bartender. Then we read, amazingly, an account of last night's Yale reading. "God, and here we sit, reading it, in Lowell," he marveled, "and where's Jack?"

At that moment, in came Nick—big-faced, bluff, blue-suited, with large somehow heavy eyes, the eyes of a tired, harried man dealing with some bad turning that his life had taken; the talkative, assertive, helpful, bearlike brother, who was at home in the loquacities of winter-taverns. Stella, he said, was outside in the car. So out we all went. Only Allen had ever met her, because when Jack came to New York or Connecticut he always came alone.

There in the frigid street, with the wind at our backs, and the northern dusk coming down with the implacability of a shroud, she looked up as Nick opened the car door, as startled as a bird but knowing for a certainty who we were, and got out—so much smaller than I had imagined, with a strong-featured, intense face, a wide mouth, and bright black eyes that filled with tears at the sight of us (no, the eyes sprung tears against the mind's instructions), and she choked on a sob as if she'd been struck in the stomach, and got out, "All of you here! *Why* didn't you come to Florida when he needed you?" with a tone of fierce, involuntary recrimination that was followed immediately by a kiss for Shirley, and then for each of us in turn, because we'd been his friends, and had come to his funeral, after all.

I leaned over and kissed her hand, and a smile-crooked, brave, and somehow worse than the tears—managed to contort her mouth: "He loved you all," she said. "He never stopped talking about you," the tears welling up again, just coming of themselves, and then she looked at Gregory, and actually laughed: "Oh, Gregory, he used to talk—," shaking her head back and forth at funny stories Jack must have told her about this crazy, ex-juvenile-delinquent, Italian Shelley, who helped her back into the car, and then climbed in beside her.

We were introduced to Tony Sampas—the thin brother, the lawyer, who lived over Nicky's bar with no wife in sight, and stayed up with the difficult drunks, like Jack, and perhaps slept in a single bed in a dim room with only a bureau and a chair in it; weary, dependable Tony, who had flown down to Florida immediately, and hadn't slept in two-three days. "I'll take her over to the mother's place now," he said to me in an undertone, "and see you later . . . And, really, it means a lot to her, and all of us, that you could come."

So we all trailed back into the bar again with Nick, who took over the details of the next hours with the gruff and thoughtful ease of the best of hosts: "Now you'll have dinner right here, I'll make the dinner myself, a steak, how about steaks, and shrimp, some shrimp to start . . . No, no, you'll eat here. I set up a kitchen just last month, just for me to cook in when I feel like it, everything's taken care of . . . Now you have your drinks, anything you want . . . Walter, give them anything they want . . ."

So there we were: Shirley and I with more whiskey, Gregory having retsina, Allen and Peter sipping sherry, and all of us going back into the kitchen now and then where Nick was hauling out steaks and shrimp and lobster, and talking steadily, the big, heavy, tough, imploring eyes saying: Just don't worry, everything's taken care of, the Sampas's appreciate your coming all this way, and of course you'll stay at Mike's (still another brother, a social worker, the quieter brother, who hadn't married Greek, and somehow seemed to lack the easy, central place in the middle of the family's ambiance, and had a fifteen room house for his six kids and Protestant wife), you'll stay there, say no more about it—Why are they *protesting*? You mean, they should stay in some motel when they've come all the way up here for Jackie's funeral?

I was amazed at how difficult it was for us to simply accept the Sampas's generosity—the opening of house, pantry, purse; the giving of beds and food; the willingness to include us in the rituals of their bereavement. We were continually trying to find words to thank them, as if each of us needed to remain poised in a kind of stoic equilibrium if we were to get through, and so had withdrawn slightly into ourselves where even kindness was an intrusion. The Sampas's, on the contrary, automatically drew together in the emergency, and became a tribe once more, their differences from each other put aside for the moment, only the likenesses remaining. It came to me in the hours that followed that, as Jack had known, the primal basis for society is still the family after all, and, uprooted from its supportiveness, our individual attempts at understatement seemed a pathetic psychic orphaning. For if death is one of the great life experiences, it is precisely because it awakens all the hungers that define our mortality—the need to weep, to laugh, to touch, to help and its consolation is the reminder of human fraternity that it offers to anyone not too armored by fear to receive it. Thankfully, our "notorious" individualities melted, and we joined the group.

Dinner was spread out on a long table in the eating-half of the bar—a pile of steaks, a dish of lobster meat, shrimp, breads, a bottle of retsina—eat, eat, eat! While we did, we were occupied with the thought that we hadn't thought of flowers. There should be some from Jack's friends, from "American literature," as Allen said. So Gregory sketched out an elaborate floral symbol—a large red heart resting on a lotus, with spikes of fire shooting out of it, and five thorns with our first names on them. But what to say on the ribbon? "Hold the heart," Allen suggested. Then the end of *Mexico City Blues* came to mind, and I said: "No, guard the heart. Or, he guarded the heart."

"Maybe it's too military?" Gregory wondered.

Later, the lotus, and the spikes of fire, and even the thorns, proved impossible for the florist to create at that late hour, but a large heart of red roses was made for us, with white roses around it, and ribbons with our names on them, and these names added, because they were close friends of Jack's: Lucien (Carr), Bill (Burroughs), and Robert (Creeley). And in the center, *Guard the Heart.*

After eating, we sat in the bar, waiting to go to the funeral home. A flush-faced, sandy-haired young man, with the look of an ex-basketballer starting to lose his muscle tone to the beer, was hunched over a drink a stool away, and Nick insisted that we meet him, because he had gotten drunk with Jack so many times. He shook hands with each of us gravely, and said: "He was something, though, wasn't he? I mean, I'm no slouch with the sauce myself, but Jack—" shaking his head at Jack's prodigious thirst, his red-rimmed eyes sobered with shock.

I thought: How many hundreds of guys there must be who had gone along on historic, days-long binges with Jack, and told the stories over and over ever since, not because Jack was Jack Kerouac, but because he was a boozer's boozer, and something always happened, something uproarious or outlandish or mind-boggling, that often ended in the ludicrous jailtank in the ashes of dehydrated dawn. How many there must be who felt they were his good old buddies, because they had known the surprising intimacy and candor of his cups, and remembered that florid, volatile face yelling or laughing, playing the records on any juke, telling them with feckless exuberance, "Hey, I'm Jack Kerouac," but never giving too much of a damn whether they'd heard of him or not, because it was a great night, it was a good place, let's go somewhere else, let's find us a mad goddamn party. And how many had fastened on him just *because* he was Jack Kerouac—"Hey, man, you know who I got stoned with last night? Jack fucking-well *Kerouac!* Yah, you know, the Beat writer! I'm going to drive him up into New England someplace next week." How many had laughed *with* him (or at him) and spent *his* money (or their own) and passed out to his voice still indefatigably trying to keep pace with the reel of his imagination, but never heard the drowning note of maddened fatalism that had blurred it recently.

These were the people among whom Jack had spent a lot of his last years—bar-flies, mechanics with a Saturday-night-thirst, the jocks around the local saloon, tyro writers talking their books away, the punks-of-the-night looking for a latch to build tomorrow on, the wifeless, overworked, bored, sweat-socked men and boys of bewildered inner-America, who could recognize a certified roarer and his roll. These kept him company, and with them he burned up his intelligence in the conflagration of those boozy monologues over a scarred bartop.

Why did he drink like that? I think it was because his was a deeply traditional nature, so sensitive to social and familial cohesions, and their breakdown in the modern world, that he intuited more about the contemporary human mood in his nerves and mind than anyone I had ever known. And yet most of his close friends were alienated, rootless urban-types, and so he lived simultaneously in both worlds, a tremulous bridge between two realities bent on denying one another, a seismograph trying to register an earthquake in the middle of a tornado—and drink temporarily seemed to stabilize his psychic ground. He drank, as well, because he had no gift for even a saving cynicism, and couldn't act out the simplest role (much less the infinitely complex role of "spokesman" or "prophet"), and because, though he was the most insatiably gregarious man when tipsy, he was not easily sociable when sober, and increasingly, as he got older, was occupied with the enigma of his own identity ("I'm descended from an Iroquois Chief," he would announce. "I'm a Breton nobleman," he would insist a week later), and finally he drank because I don't think he wanted to live anymore if there was no place to direct his kind of creative drive, except inward. But I don't really know. All I know for sure is that it has pained *this* head for years to imagine the waste to him of those thousand barroom nights, and that something must be awry in an America where a man of such human richness, and such extraordinary gifts, would be most appropriately mourned in a hundred saloons because he felt he had no other place to go-the fraternal warmth for which his whole soul longed having been exiled to the outer edges of life in the America of his time.

While we waited, Gregory went upstairs to shave, because in the car Stella had said: "Comb your hair, take a shave—do it for Jack," and as he went off, he said: "I'll shave for Jack, for Jack's woman, but damn it, when I'm ninety they're still going to want to cut my hair, shave me, dress me up—when I'm *ninety*! Oughtn't a man to know the way he wants to be, and be left to it, when he's ninety?"

Then we were off to Archambault's Funeral Home, with Nick directing us, rolling down empty streets of small-city American neon, with cracked sidewalks down which one imagined *Doctor Sax*'s manuscript "riffling" in the winter wind, which was how Jack had gleefully described it to me once outside the San Remo in the Village on a night as cold, when we were both in our twenties and bursting with Melville, five years before he wrote the book: "And then, see, this manuscript comes *riffling* down the sidewalk out of nowhere—this tenible, prophetic testament of what lies at the end of the night!"—a manuscript which (it had always seemed to me) Jack had spent the rest of his life transcribing out of the original version.

Funeral homes are all alike, of course. Archambault's was Victorian in decor, with pale green walls, lofty ceilings, an ornate balustrade going up from the vestibule to—what? The formaldehyde rooms. The butcher shops. Wherever it was they stored the coffins, and showed them to customers susceptible in their bereavement. Two "showings" were going on in opposite rooms, and the neatly-lettered placards (like those in hotel-lobbies telling you in which room your convention is being held) announced "Kerouac" on the left and "Levesque" on the right.

The Kerouac room was filled with people—middle-class, well-dressed Lowell people, and a few kids (Custer-bearded youths with grave, out-of-place faces, and mini-skirted girls, solemn with they knew-not-what unclear emotions). Most of the local people seemed to be Sampas relatives, and suddenly I realized how few Kerouacs there had ever been. Later, we met a row of young Kerouac second cousins—pretty little girls with that dark, round-faced Breton look, and muscular, abashed boys from Dracut or Nashua. Among the crowd was Charley, the eldest Sampas, news-editor of the *Lowell Sun*, a large, suave man with flesh on him, in a well-cut business suit, balding now, the successful head of the clan, his urbane eyes on all the details. It was Charley who had encouraged Jack to write when Jack was best friends with his younger brother, Sebastian, who had been killed in Europe in 1944. Charley had told Jack that if he wanted to write he ought to get out of Lowell, and perhaps Charley, too, had wanted something more than to be standing there in his expensive suit, with certain private ambitions unachieved despite his position in the community. We met further Sampas relatives, and friends, and friends of friends, most of them Greeks in that French funeral home, and there, too, was Stella on a settee off to one side, out of the theatrical lights that bathed the coffin, and the banks of fresh flowers, and—Jack.

Down to it, I didn't much want to "view" whatever some mortician had thought to fashion out of what was left of him, but I knew I would. Allen and Peter and Gregory went right up through the crowd to have a look, but whether they had seen the handiwork of funeral homes before I didn't know. Allen and Peter had observed dozens of corpses on the burning ghats in India, but (as Allen said later) that was natural, you see the husk of the body for what it is—organs, so much simple meat, just the garbage of our crysallis from which the butterfly has flown, nothing but the residue of transitory life. But in the war, I had seen half-a-hundred dead sailors being gotten ready for shipping home to inconsolable parents and wives, and later "viewed" my father laid out under the lights like a waxwork-figure in Madame Tussaud's that is somehow *unlike* the person precisely because cold skill has so striven to make it resemble them, feature to feature, and you stand in utter perplexity wondering why it doesn't, only to become aware that what is missing is not merely movement, animation, but something else, the invisible spark that makes the mask cohere, the soul lighting up the persona from within, the unique and irreplaceable Being that invests the face with human possibilities.

Anyway, I pushed my way through the crowd alone, fearful I might be revulsed and that it would all come down on me if anything of Jack was actually there, and over the dark silhouette of a shoulder, I saw him—laid out in flowers, in the prescribed funerary attitude of tranquil slumber, hands folded with a rosary entwined, in a pale shirt, a natty bow-tie, and a sport-jacket. No need to say that no one had ever seen him that way since he was Harcourt Brace's soulful young Thomas Wolfe twenty years before. And the face? It had been made to look as peaceful as a babe, the brows slightly knotted but with perplex rather than pain, all the fevers gone, the mouth not his mouth at all, the color of the flesh a rather pale pink in the lights, Jack's sweaty, grinning, changeable expression nowhere to be seen. He looked thin, calm, waxen, almost choir-boyish—and Jack had once been choir-boyish allright—but this was a faintly prissy, I'm-allright-Jack Jack, and no Jack I'd ever known. Later, Allen would say: "I stood there, and suddenly I expected him to *wink*. That is, the Jack that was watching all of us watching him would have made that eyelid wink to tell us that everything was all just so much vapor circling upwards in the void."

Gregory was kneeling at one side of the coffin, crying now, and I remembered the easy, public tears of Italy, the bawling men coming back from Venice's burial island in the dignity of a grief that is openly acknowledged, and I looked at Jack again, and felt for just a moment the sheer obscenity of death, the irreparable period that it places at the end of portions of our lives, closing us off forever from the consciousness that has gone, and the first sick feeling of gut-loss came over me. "It will be different to write from now on . . .": the words came back, and I hoped that no one would ever mourn me so self-centeredly. Tears welled up into my eyes, the involuntary tears that we sometimes shed for the mute flesh itself. He wouldn't walk, he wouldn't run, he wouldn't ever come into my house again, yelling like a banshee, or grinning pensively, or moody with his special thoughts. That's what I felt. His body died before my eyes, and I had to accept that I was stuck in my own body, in my own flesh, and that this mannequin was the last I'd see of a friend of twenty-one years of feverish association. I put an arm around Gregory, and we turned away.

I found Shirley, who had taken only the briefest look from a distance, and we went up to Stella, who broke down again as we bent over her, and Shirley knelt down and stayed with her for a while after I'd muttered a futile word or two, hugged her, and cursed under my breath. Cursed what? My own closed throat that wanted to bring up something consoling, something that wouldn't push her over any further—all that grief-role crap which, like joy-role crap, is only crap, after all. Better to stumble out: Jack's *dead!* What am I going to *do!* But instead trying for control, trying not to say a word that would trigger emotions neither of us could afford. And all the while her eyes observed me, something going on behind her tears: "Is *this* John Holmes? Is this Jack's friend? Why isn't he suffering? Is he suffering? What kind of suffering is that?"

Hours, hours—the room too hot—too many people to meet—too many names to remember. After a while, Shirley and I went down into the Smoking Lounge (oh, the imaginations of morticians, all of whom aspire to the respectability of theater-managers), where we sat and smoked and talked about other things and kept each other company. Then, coming down the stairs, I saw a face I recognized, but couldn't place for a second. It was Ann Charters, who had compiled Jack's bibliography a few years before. She was wearing a large, knitted tam and a chic suede coat, and her alert, intelligent face, with the observant eyes and quick smile, was pale with cold, and her husband, Sam, whom I'd never met, was with her. He was a big, handsome man in a stylish, box-back overcoat, with the longish hair of someone older "on the scene"; a poet and a producer of Rock records, who exuded a sense of physical health, and the natural optimism of someone who is usually too busy to mope.

We all started chattering at once (death makes you talk, you talk so as not to think, you chatter as if you'd found a similar soul at the worst cocktail party of all time), and at one point Sam said: "I re-read your Kerouac chapter in *Nothing More To Declare* the other night, and it's the best thing on Jack so far." I felt a curious twinge in my gut, but didn't recognize what it was, except that it wasn't just my old reflex of being unable to accept praise. "You should do the *book*," Sam said."There's going to be a book, and you're probably the one to do it." *Twinge.* Later, the next afternoon, Sterling Lord, Jack's literary agent and mine, would say to me: "You know, John, you're really the one to do the *book*. You knew him from the inside, you were there when so much of it happened, but you can stand away from it all, too." *Twinge.* "No, really, you're the one to do it," and the twinge became knowledge. The idea of the *book*—that combination of authorized biography and cool critical assessment without which America does not know how to think about its most challenging writers—revolted me. It seemed a coffin no less inadequate to contain the Jack I'd known than the one in which he lay.

I didn't want to go through it all again. I didn't want to have to rifle my own memories, much less other people's and try to be objective, measured, scholarly. I realized that I had loved him because, on an entirely private level, I had understood his point of view with an instant-empathy that was the closest thing to clairvoyance in my life, and the goddamn *book* would have to be done by someone other than this survivor of the last, maddening quarter-century, who had his own secrets, bad habits, awful mornings of hangover, resolutions to save himself, arduous days of getting through on nothing but nerve, futile hopes for two months' rest, for a calm life once the fever eased, for mint-fresh mornings of zestful work. For I *did* know why Jack drank. We talked to each other sometimes late at night, utterly different men with a similar cast of mind, the same wound in the heart, and he talked to me as an alcoholic in the Age of Pot. "How glum life is without the booze," he said to me once, raising his glass mockingly, able to say it right out to me, knowing I would understand just what it was made men like us feel glum—our disappointed expectations, and the novelist's necessity to accept into his work the irreconcilables that his own personal hopes struggle to deny.

When we went back upstairs, people were starting to drift out of the "viewing" room, leaving Stella there, kneeling by Jack, caressing his face, kissing him, a hunched, small, abandoned figure in the theatrical lights, her shoulders heaving just a little.

We crowded into the car again to go to the Sampas's mother's house for "the wake," Nick coming along with us to give directions, Peter navigating through the narrow, rutted streets of residential Lowell, and missing turns because Nick was always craning over his shoulder to talk to those of us in back (patient Peter "uh-*huh*-ing" when corrected), to stop on a corner under a few spare trees, on a block of plain old commodious houses, with an empty lot across the street, and a shuttered factory beyond a chain link fence. We piled out and went into the house across a small veranda.

It was already overcrowded with people. There was a baby-grand in the front hall, off of which was a pin-neat parlor with doilies on the chair-arms and landscapes on the walls. Beyond was the TV room with a butt-sprung couch and a wall of photographs—Nick in his Army tunic, Mike as a young student, Sebastian in the central spot—a thin, beaming young man in uniform, with curly blondish hair, looking out of the Forties at this night. The kitchen was full of dark, heavily attractive women bustling about a large, restaurant-size coffee urn, and shoo-ing everyone out. A sumptuous spread was laid out on the dining room table—*feta* in chalk-white wedges, heaping plates of pastries, slices of delicious spinach-pie, and cup on cup of coffee.

The house was too small for all the people who milled around the immense, two-hundred-and-fifty pound Sampas matriarch, who spoke little English, and wheezed down into sagging armchairs in her bedroom slippers, and was brought food and drink by other, aging Greek ladies. Stella sat among these women, attended by her friends from long-ago highschool days, looking at everything as if from a new, strange distance—at the warm, thronged circle of Jack's Lowell (and her own) within which moved his curious friends from the disordered city-years—her eyes asking herself: Can all this be true? When will I wake up?

We ate and drank coffee, and Gregory came up to me with that day's copy of the *Harvard Crimson* that had an obituary. "John, you've gotta read this . . . this says it all." What it said was what I had seen on the faces of the Yalies the night before, and in the bewildered young men at the funeral home: We don't know exactly why it's such a shock. We never really read him much. But today we realize that he meant something to us after all, and we don't know why he's dead. And this curious last line: "We should say a prayer for him: God give us strength to be as alive as Kerouac was. Send us more to help burn away the bullshit."

A word about this matter of the kids—the hippies, the activists, the *children* of the Beats. The next day they were at the church, and again at the cemetery, in their scruffy duds and Franz Joseph wings of sideburn, each with a camera clicking away, getting "shots," as if they were recording an event the meaning of which would only become clear in the developer, and most of them seemed to have been impelled to come for reasons that they only began to comprehend once there. They all looked as if this was their first funeral, and they were uneasy about being that close to the death they talked and sang about so much. They were interviewed continually by newsmen from Boston or New York, who sensed a sure-fire human interest story here (NOW GENERATION TALKS ABOUT FATHER OF BEATS), but I don't think most of them had thought very much about Kerouac in the last few years. They had probably read *On The Road*, or one of the easier books, when they were fifteen or sixteen, and had written him off in the light of his recent political statements, tuned out by his unfashionable love of his country, and his disinterest in their subculture and its heroes. And yet they came.

At the cemetery, I overheard a young reporter from *Rolling Stone* say to Sterling Lord: "Well, it was his politics—I mean, we can't relate to all that America shit," and I heard myself break in, and say: "Don't understand him too easily. His politics began on another level than yours." But how could I say what I meant? The Jack who came out for William Buckley, who occasionally was about as intolerant as Archie Bunker, and sometimes skirted perilously close to Anti-semitism—how could I say that he really wasn't that way? "Allright, smartass," the young man could have quite reasonably demanded, "what's your evidence?" There was nothing I could say but this: *I know in my heart the man wasn't that way.*

I had argued with him over issues for twenty years, only to realize that politics weren't real to him at all, convinced, as he was, that most "issues" were evasions of our actual human complicity, and that truth lay elsewhere—down in what Yeats had called "the foul rag-and-bone shop of the heart." Also, he had the impatience with logic, and the cartwheeling leaps of insight, that sometimes characterize the alcoholic mind. But above all, he was a lonely, disappointed man, who had been down all the roads—the drugs, the screws, the fantasies, the highs, the hopes—and knew in his own ravaged nerves what was left at "the end of the night." Beyond that, I think he felt emotionally disenfranchised by the polarization of an America that no longer seemed to care about the urge towards harmony that he believed to be its founding truth.

It was too soon to say that he was wrong, and so I said nothing more to the young man from *Rolling Stone*. Still, the presence of those kids at his funeral leads me to conclude that the obit in the *Crimson* accurately reflected a feeling of mysterious kinship which Jack's sudden death aroused in so many of the young.

The evening inched along with exquisite slowness. We were all depleted, our brains numbed remembering names, and some of us longed for a drink, and others for sleep, and finally Stella got up and padded through the crowds without a word, and went to bed. We stayed on for a while, and then piled into the car again, and went on to Mike's house, following the red eye of his tail-light.

The house was a large, three-storied, Victorian mansion with a *porte-cochere*, in a style that might be dubbed "Mill-owner New England." We brought our bags and our weary eyes into a huge, dark-paneled kitchen. Betty, Mike's wife, the Protestant girl from Marietta, Ohio (her direct, hospitable nature shaped by the splendid curve of the river there, as particular rivers shape the natures of those who live beside them)—was chubby, good looking, a no-nonsense nestler of children, quietly observant, the kind of woman who likes to sink down in an easy chair after the day is over and have a convivial drink with her husband. She had been around most of the evening, pleasant but unobtrusive, keeping in the background the way an "outsider" in a large, tight-knit, boisterous family usually does. But now she was in her own house, and she got out drinks while Mike took us up to the third floor and our rooms.

We went up through the enormous house with its twelve foot ceilings and heavily varnished woodwork, its black and gold marble mantels and ornate brass fixtures in the bathrooms. Two little boys were sleeping so soundly in one room that even our tramping through didn't cause them to stir, and there were two little girls in another room amid a profusion of dolls and Twiggy-posters, and there was Tony, the son of twelve, who had his room up on the third floor near ours. It was a jumble of hi-fi, flower-power, Charlie Brown, and, lo, a huge Allen Ginsberg poster-photo" The boy was giddy with the idea that *he* was actually in his very own house, and you could feel his impatience for tomorrow, and school, and his buddies. Allen promptly whipped out a pen and wrote his name, and a line or two, on the poster.

Downstairs, the fifteen year old daughter, a self-contained young creature with a fall of fine brown hair on her shoulders, and a pretty, coltish face, sat with us in one of the parlors as, exhausted, we finally had a big drink with her parents. Peter had resolutely gone off to bed, and Gregory got himself a drink and went off too. Allen sat with Shirley on a couch, I sank into a large armchair to savor the taste of the bourbon on gums anesthetized by too many cigarettes, and we talked of death, the girl listening gravely, saying little or nothing, but very adult in her attention.

"It's really strange," Allen said. "With all of you, all of this, all Lowell . . . Do you think it mightn't have happened if he'd stayed here instead of moving down to Florida?"

"Well, we could have at least protected him a little," Mike said. "I mean, you know, the police all knew him here, and we'd go down and get him out of jail when he went on a binge. We could have looked after him . . . We shouldn't have let his mother insist on the move. I mean, Jack and Stella didn't really want to go down there. He wrote Tony just about two weeks ago that somehow they'd come back in the Spring. We didn't do enough, I guess—," this solemn, worried man, resembling none of the other Sampas's (none of whom resembled each other, as if the loins of the parents had contained whole tribes), with his dark brows of puzzled concern, his bony nose; a man kept thin with worry as his wife got plump with childbearing; an upright man worried about his responsibility to the death of a crazy brother-in-law.

"Well," Allen said, "I was interested to see his face. Did anyone think to take a picture of him?" This tightened my gut a little, but I understood Allen's long view, and time makes most proprieties seem silly. "I heard from Ann Charters," he went on, "that some of his papers and some photos were burned. Do you know what he wrote just before the hemorrhage? The papers said he wrote something . . . And by the way, I really think one of his friends should be a pall-bearer."

I, too, was worried about Jack's meticulously preserved record of his life, his countless notebooks, sketchbooks, journals, and fugitive jottings-on-the-road. I, too, felt that one of us, one of Jack's friends, should help bear his pall, but rejected Allen's notion that we draw lots, and insisted that he be the one, being the oldest friend among us, and he accepted the suggestion. But I was bone-weary too, and gulped a quick second drink, and Shirley and I went off to bed up under the eaves of that many-chambered house, opening the shutters of one window to look briefly out at the fierce stars burning over New Hampshire, under which Jack and I had discovered that we had both walked (me, along the Pemigewassett River; he, along the Merrimack into which it flowed) on the same windy night after the big flood of 1937—only one of the many odd coincidences (like the fact that we had been born on the same day in March) that had lent our friendship a special, brotherly quality. I hung my corduroys from the top bureau drawer so that some semblance of press might remain for tomorrow, and climbed into the firm Victorian bed under the warm weight of three cotton blankets, and slept like the dead until seven the next morning.

THREE

Which dawned fair and milder than the day before, with tall, white, supple birches outside that high window. I shaved as Shirley packed us up. Probably we wouldn't be corning back here. Allen had to go to New York that night, and he would be driving into Logan with the Charters'. Peter and Gregory would go back to the farm with Robert Creeley, who was coming over from Rochester for the funeral. We would just go on home.

Down in the kitchen, two of Jack's friends from Albany were going into their 20th hour awake. I'd seen them the night before at the Sarnpas' house, and afterwards, as it turned out, they'd gone to the bars to mourn and carouse, and now they had turned up here at Mike's for coffee and some of Betty's French toast. One, a massive, tousled-haired man, who knew he looked as poetic and virile as the early Brendan Behan, had a barrel-chest like Jack's of recent years. He had run a bar in Florida where Jack drank, and then he had moved back North to go into teaching. With him was a knotty, walnut-faced little psychiatrist, who rambled on continually in a raspy, cigarette-roughened voice, telling stories he had told too many times before. Betty cooked, and listened, her copious hair let down over the shoulders of her kimona.

Allen appeared, his face scoured by sleep, not a psychic burr on him, and had a cup of tea. Gregory came down muzzily, and sipped a light whiskey for his tooth. We were due at the funeral home at ten, as it turned out, so that the cars could be properly lined up for the procession to the church. I had hoped to go out for a walk on my own, just to get the air, to sniff out Lowell-ambiance, to look at trees, but there wasn't going to be time. Suddenly, in fact, it was ten of ten, and Peter was awakened with only time to gulp a quick mug of coffee while Gregory loaded his camera, and we were off.

Morning Lowell reminded me of Fall River or New Bedford—trampled school-lots full of children, factories a-smoke, the mild air of autumn amid the yellowing trees. The street in front of Archambault's was full of funeral directors in grey-suede gloves, striped trousers, and the self-satisfied faces of traffic-managers in communion with the mysteries of logistics. We were gotten into the line, and went inside.

It was just like the night before, except that a pale-yellow, Chekhovian sun bathed the room where Jack lay in his waxen, musing pose. Gregory took movies to the silent shock of Sampas's, and Shirley and I sat in the vestibule, waiting. Then our names were called, and we went back to the car again, Gregory lingering behind to get "shots" of the coffin coming out, Allen to ride in the pallbearers' car. We waited again, Peter (good Peter, without breakfast, in need of more coffee, still at the wheel of my cold car) watching for Gregory in the rear-view mirror. When he came, we pulled out into the line, and rolled slowly towards the church.

There were cops and funeral directors in the narrow street, people were thronging up the wide steps to the cathedral, a wan sun gilded the brick-red upper stories of commercial buildings. We double-parked in the line, and got out, and queued-up with the "family & friends"—who, according to the logistics, were to troop in solemnly at the last moment, like actors in a mystery-play as it might have been written by Samuel Beckett. Moving along, there was Sterling Lord at the bottom of the steps, natty as ever in his blue shirt with the white collar and a dark necktie, with his encouraging eyes behind the glasses, and his reticent half-smile betraying the sensitivity of a decent man to the unknown emotions of others; Sterling who had known Jack in such a different way than most of us—as an agent, but as *Jack's* agent, which meant no chilly professionalism, for Jack put his head, as well as his work, into your hands. He came forward, and we shook hands on the occasion, and I wanted to stop a moment, but, no, we were urged on—logistics again!—up the steps and through a high portal into the church itself. Inside, it was all lofty light, pale marble columns, dark-wood pews, the stained glass windows over the altar-blue and green and red in the lovely sun-depicting saints in the tall, Greco-esque majesty of their robes.

We were led down to a point just behind the pews reserved for the family, and Shirley (shrouded in a black-lace scarf that had materialized out of her purse) pulled down the knee-rest automatically, ex-Catholic as she was, and all at once I could feel her grief. She was tensing towards the austere words of the Mass that would finalize it all for her. There was no help for her now, she was going to have to endure that celebration of the mystery of Death, from which the renegade-Catholic can flee, but never far enough, and she couldn't just "get through it" as I could. The fact was going to be nailed down in her consciousness. She and Jack had been lapsed-Catholics together, they had had that between them like the stoicism of cigarette-smokers who accept the cancer-statistics but refuse to quit, and so much else too—a certain bantering camaraderie, a line-perfect memory for the lyrics of all the songs, an unspoken acknowledgement of the frailty behind life's poses, *me*. To Shirley, I knew, Jack's death had been an inevitability, not because of the booze (she was married to a boozer of sorts, she'd nursed my groanings, she'd learned to accept the prodigious thirsts of a secret idealist whose private motto was *Break the Black Heart*), but because down in herself she believed that the best of life came down to this. She believed that there was a mortality that tracked every one of us out of season. She was a soldier who was revulsed by the war of life but stubbornly wouldn't desert it. She had that toughness that only comes from certain bitter acceptances made when one is too young to recognize the sadder, more ambivalent options, and she had learned to hold onto people, who were special to her, with open hands—and Jack had been special to her in a way that had little to do with me. And now the ritual of the Mass, which would have been a catharsis for the devout, promised her nothing but the cold clarities and losses of the morgue.

The coffin and the pall-bearers came down past us (Allen there, with his beard, and duffel coat, and shoulder-slung bag) and the Mass began. It was a High Requiem Mass, performed in English, with the priest facing *us* instead of the altar, but I couldn't concentrate on it. I got up and stood, I sat when others sat, I listened to the chants, the responses, and registered none of it. I stared at the coffin, and thought of Jack inside it. The priest, an old friend of Jack's of whom I'd heard stories for twenty years, gave the eulogy, a good eulogy too (in my doubter's troubled mind I thought it a good job of work), and I got up and stood dumb in my shoes, and sat down, and couldn't pray, but said the words of the Lord's Prayer when it came, and honestly hoped their hope, thinking that Jack's hunger for continuity, Jack's essential reverence, was being well-served. Then communion. Because most of the people there were Greeks, only a few took it—one, a lank-haired Ippolit, hurried up late, as if responding to a sudden impuse. And at last Shirley wept.

Then it was finished, the priest circling the casket with the swaying censer, as his "helper" held his robes back from the candles. The funeral directors came up, genuflecting automatically with the wheeze of too many lavish dinners, sheparding the pall-bearers to their proper places, and we filed out, down the long aisle behind Stella and the family, out into the sun again where photographers jumped about, and Allen stood next to the hearse being interviewed, a crisp wind ruffling his beard there in the traffic-jammed street.

Sterling came down the steps with Jimmy Breslin, whom I'd never met, and we stood there in the crowd, and talked for a minute. "Jimmy came up with me," Sterling said with his wide smile. "He didn't think I should come up by myself." Breslin had that sober, tousled, knotted look of a man who is sharing other people's loss, people who might not know how to get through a ritual that he understands in his very gristle, and I liked him instantly. Then, suddenly, there was Robert Creeley, too—wiry as a guitar string, and graceful, with the meticulous small beard of a bravo or a cavalier, in a proper suit and short overcoat, his one busy eye saying, "Yes. At last. Funny. Well. We all *do* exist, after all," as we were introduced.

We piled into the car in a maze of photographers, among them Gregory, who'd gotten more "perfect shots," and again moved off in the procession, Creeley coming along with us. There was nothing to say, and so we chatted. Peter drove, and I lit cigarettes for him, and Shirley commented on the brevity of the new Mass, and I thought about these streets every name of which I'd known for two decades, and it seemed to be miles before we reached the cemetery gates where the line of cars paused, then moved on, then came to a stop at last. We got out into the musing, somber air that New England graveyards exude, the leaves drifting amid old stones and meandering walks, and there, beyond some trees, across a strip of macadam, a green canopy had been raised over the fresh-dug grave.

Brief ceremonies, ceremonial words to which I didn't listen. The late October breeze stirred in the elms, the crowds milled, photographers posed getting poses. But no ceremonies ease the sight of a coffin poised over a grave's raw hole, and Stella stood there before it, shrouded now in widow's veils, her arm held by Charlie, the eldest, as the last stark prayer was said.

Then there was a rush to grab flowers and toss them on the casket. I looked on, a few steps away. Allen and Peter and Gregory were selecting roses from our flower-heart, red roses that they laid on the burnished bronze surface of the casket. I went up and took a white rose, and put it over the place where Jack's head lay.

Sterling and Allen were being "set up" for a TV interview (great shot: Ginsberg talking about Kerouac, and behind him the coffin going down into the earth—"So, Mr. Ginsberg, I'll ask you to assess his career briefly, the camera's not rolling yet, but in a minute, and then you make your statement and just stand a little farther over to the left so that we can get it all in the picture.") I registered all this, but felt nothing. It seemed as meaningless as the commercials that interrupt the disasters on the TV news. The young man from *Rolling Stone* was at my elbow, asking irrelevant questions. Why did Jack drink? Was he, in my opinion, significant? What had he thought of Rock? But I was numb—even to irony.

I saw Allen and Gregory standing near the coffin that was about to be lowered, and I broke away. I didn't have another word in me. I stood with them, and the funeral-man pressed some sort of button, and, easy as grease, Jack went down into the ground. "Here, you should throw the first dirt," someone said to Allen, a strange young man in work-clothes, and Allen reached down to the pile, and clenched up a handful, and tossed it. Then Gregory, the same. It was hard to get a real handful because of the stones. Then me. I took up the stones too, and open-handed them down on Jack's head.

Confusion, milling again. I stood around and didn't know what to do. Shirley stayed on the edges of the crowd, which was dispersing now. Breslin had gone back to the rented Cadillac in which he and Sterling had come from Boston airport. Creeley looked on with a cold eye, doing it his own way. We all tarried, and then turned to leave, but the gravediggers were spading the dirt down onto the casket, joking to each other (which was apt somehow, workmen doing, as they do, the dirty jobs, and not making too much of it), so we turned back there under the cold, fluttering trees, and watched the pile of earth fill the hole. I don't know why we all turned back at the same time—some last awareness of what was being sealed off from us by the spades, I suppose. And then we'd all had enough, and drifted back to the car—Gregory and Peter and Shirley and Bob Creeley and me scuffling through the leaves, back to the car in the graphic sunlight of a perfect October day, to finish up.

There was a lighter mood in the little rooms of the Sampas's mother's house now, a mood not unmixed with that familiar upwelling of relief that follows a bad experience. There were paper cups of scotch, and cans of soda and beer, and another lavish spread—the fish that is traditional on such occasions with the Greeks, plus macaroni dishes, rolls, salads, enough for twenty more than there were of us, brought around in the crowd by those large, darkly-attractive women.

Drinks were being urged on Breslin by Nick, who was intent on introducing him to everyone: "Jimmy, want you to meet so-and-so . . . This is Jimmy—Jimmy Breslin," who, at the moment, seemed to feel that his name, and his fame too, were intrusions here. I was looking for an opportunity to talk to Stella, so I waited my time, and ate some of the good food. Then Sterling was nearby, against a wall in the dining-room with his plate, and we talked a little. No, Jack hadn't been "drinking heavily for three days" as most of the papers had it, just drinking along as usual, but he'd been feeling baddish for a month, and all of a sudden he'd started to hemmorrhage, and didn't want a doctor, but Stella had called the ambulance anyway, and they'd worked over him for hours, then his liver quit, and the surgery didn't help, and that was that. No, he probably hadn't been conscious much after he'd been taken from the house.

I drifted off to get my single drink, only to be buttonholed by the barrel-chested bar-owner from Florida, sleepy-eyed and slow-talking now. "I wonder if I could ask you—," he began, fumbling in his briefcase, and producing a manuscript. "It's only about 1,200 words . . . I've been moving words around these last months." I was speechless with the inappropriateness of the request, but it seemed easier to read it than to wrangle. I stepped outside onto the little porch, and sat in a crisp breeze, and read another half-cynical, half-sentimental version of the one story everyone tries to tell eventually: the death of a father, or brother, or mother, or wife, or friend. Years of reading snatches of fugitive manuscript under such conditions made it easy enough for me to tell at just what juncture the work failed to come off. Years of talking about writing to younger people made it possible for me to articulate at least some of this to him, and to get through the first look of confusion, and disappointment, and the blunt question, "Is it publishable?" I knew just how *little* outside comments helped if the author wasn't ready to hear them, if he hadn't reached that point where the work was more important than his own feelings about it, and how *much* they could help if he truly wanted to know what it was he had, or hadn't, done. When I was the rawest of tyros, Jack used to read my manuscripts that way, and sketch in all the levels of experience that hadn't gotten on the page. To me, it had been of inestimable help, and I'd rarely turned a manuscript away without a reading since, though one soon became aware that most of the time the young writer would be saying to his friends half an hour later: "Oh, you know these fat-headed Establishment writers . . . some bullshit about the goddamn structure . . . I mean, he took all of *five* precious minutes to read it! I never liked his stuff much anyway . . . " Nothing to do. Hundreds of such encounters had helped make Jack an impatient, opinionated man.

Anyway, I noticed that Stella was sitting near the door to the diningroom, with a friend, and I pulled away from the hurt, angry expression on that big man's face, and went up to her. She seemed put together, though again the sight of me brought tears up into her eyes, tears that acknowledged the strange situation between us: we had never met, yet there was no way for us to be reserved, polite, or cautious with one another; we had to stumble through some reference to the occurence that had brought about our meeting at last; the irony was too bald to be covered by a witticism. So we said the words: what Jack had meant to me, what I had meant to Jack. And that being over, she could brighten a little, and we could get to know one another.

"I've had a few drinks," she said, dry-eyed now, small, a fine toughness of fiber emerging. "You know, I never drank with Jack. He didn't want me to . . ." We laughed about that, because Jack had the boozer's secret disapproval of booze, he thought of it in moral terms; also he tended to idealize women, and fall back on what he believed to be their greater resiliency and common sense.

Those last days—I'd never know the fun they'd had together! The Met's pennant run, the Series. He'd taught her to play chess, she'd taught him to play poker. They'd done a lot of sitting around. He hadn't wanted to leave the house much. And that place, St. Pete—it was no town for younger people. A funeral parlor across the street, one down on the next corner. Jack hadn't known anyone there. It was only because of his mother that they'd ever moved from Lowell. She shook her head, able not to say some of the things that were stirring up in her, able to suggest them, contained now. "But those vultures!" she said suddenly. "The people who came around to see the famous writer . . . You know how Jackie could never say, 'No.' And they'd say, even to his face, 'I'm gonna use you, you ol' bastard!' You know—supposedly joking, but they *weren't* joking."

I'd seen it, particularly in the first days after *On The Road* appeared: the curious mixture of adulation and resentment that a certain kind of celebrity seems to bring out in others; that combination of sycophancy and petulance that demands attention, or they'll conclude you're swell-headed; all the energy and exacerbated ego of the idle and purposeless who see a famous writer having a drink at a bar, and figure that writer has nothing better to do than go to a party, or on a three-day bat, or drive to Cincinnati on a whim. I'd lost Jack often enough in the early stages of an evening because he'd been drawn away into all that swirl of nerves and wastage and anticipated kicks. He had never learned to conserve himself, not if the story was interesting enough, or the person seemed to have anything unique in his spiel, or there was some promise of gaudy forgetfulness for a few hours. And, all the time, he was burning up the strengths that enabled him to keep upright in the yawning contradictions of his nature.

Stella's friend expressed concern about her finances, and she said: "Well, I can always go into the factories if I have to . . . As long as Memère is taken care of . . ." The friend thought she could probably lecture about Jack if she wanted to, but something hard came up into her face: "I'll never do that," she said harshly. "I'll never use him that way. No, *never*," her voice fiercely jealous of her private memories, as if she could already feel Literary History making its unseemly claims on them.

I crouched at her feet, and we talked some more for a while, not about Jack, but about other things, nothings, getting a little acquainted, studying one another, discovering that, yes, we liked each other. It was a moment of that brief, intense comminglement between strangers that death sometimes makes possible.

Then Sterling was there. He had to make his plane, she wasn't to worry about money. Breslin bent down, almost ceremonially, with some embarrassment, and I heard the survivor of a dozen Irish wakes say: "Sorry to meet you on this day," and he turned from Stella, and he and I shook hands without a word.

It was getting late, nearly three o'clock, and there was all that road ahead, and we had to get Allen and the others together to go back to Mike Sampas' to pick up their things. We started circulating through the rooms, saying our goodbyes. We had been warmed by them all, we had been welcomed. And perhaps the difficult acceptance of Jack's death had become less difficult for all of us because we had been together. I'd often thought that it was this older, simpler communion, this natural flow of emotions outwards from one's self, that Jack had looked for so tirelessly in his contemporaries. Now, of course, like so much in his life, something like it had emerged among the young in America, but emerged, for him, too late. They were forming communes, and the spiritual perspectives, the religious ecstacies, of which he had written, were the common coinage of these endeavors. Visionary drugs, music as group-sacrament, the non-violent witness to the holiness of all sentient life—all this had surfaced as he knew it would, and, far from being derided in the Media or patronized by the Academy (as had happened in his case), it was being heralded as the unique culture of a New Age. And Jack? Jack had dropped out of it, and been ignored by it, and grown querulous with drink and age, embittered by the unrelenting indifference to the scope and intention of his life's work, so that when he died the *New York Times* had had to call me up, asking if I could direct their obit-man to a sober, critical assessment of that work, and I had to say that I didn't know of a single one, and that (aside from his friends) I had never met anyone who had read the entire, vast cycle of the books. He remained an essentially unknown element in our literature.

I felt the parting with Stella keenly now, because perhaps better than anyone, she had known the loneliness and anger and physical horror of his last years, and I wanted her to know I knew. I told her straight out, and embraced her, and we left.

Outside in the trampled little yard, Gregory was horsing around with the loquacious psychiatrist and the bartender-cum-teacher-cum-writer, and I knew he wanted more, and didn't want it all to end, and was being lured (by the promise of bottles and talk and high jinks) to drive back to Albany with them. Jack would have felt the same. Tony Sampas took my arm. Exhaustion had drained his face like a balloon with a slow leak, his shirt collar hung around his neck loosely, and once more he thanked us for coming—this perceptive man who took on the dirty jobs stoically.

"My God, Tony," I said, "where else would we have been today?"

"I'll see you all later," Gregory said to Allen. "I'm going on . . . John, I'm gonna get down to work from now on, write poems, no more 'green armpits' stuff. We'll all meet among the buffalos," and he gave me a big, giggling suck of a kiss on the neck, and we drove off.

Back at Mike's, we collected everything. The Charters were parked in the street, waiting to take Allen to Logan. We said goodbye to good, worried Mike, and calm Betty with her arms full of little children, and waved at the Charters, and had started down the driveway when I realized that I hadn't said goodbye to Allen, and craned out the window with my hand raised, yelling, "Goodbye, man!" There he was, with the pale-gold light of mid-afternoon shining on that high, sallow dome of forehead, waving, and calling out, "Goodbye, John. Stay sweet!" This was the way it usually happened with us. We stood side by side, we chattered, we got distracted, and then lost one another in confusions, with too much left unsaid. There was never time.

I drove Bob Creeley and Peter back to the cathedral where Creeley's car was parked, and we said our so-longs. We were all, I think, feeling an unusual warmth towards each other, that warmth that puts a sense of twilight into some moments in life as you inexorably get older and come to accept that now you expect less, and the feeling passed between us. The last thing I saw was Peter's day-glo hat disappearing behind a car.

Shirley and I drove home without a break through a crisp, gathering dusk of reds and golds, the sinking sun drawing the sap up into the last of the day, that apple-tang of late autumn elusive as leaf-smoke in the air. We were quiet and close, and we found a letter from Don Wallis, an ex-student of mine, when we finally opened our door, a letter that said in part: "I came to see what I had always, I think, sensed: that Kerouac was a true and magnificent ORIGINAL whose vision of America was a true and magnificent one, at least for me; that thing I keep going back to, whenever Nixon & company drive me to it, is something of the open-souled country that lives in Kerouac and is alive fighting to get free throughout the land. For you who knew this long ago, and knew him, and knew all along the stupid & careless neglect or willed mis-reading he got from most everyone, I am sure his death is that much harder to accept . . ." And, yes, that's true, but accept it I do, because the only alternative is a bitterness that demeans the spirit a man must serve, or a grief that belittles the love he feels. And accept it I can, because I finally had my own private wake once we got back, and decided to write up this account when I felt I could.

Words? Sometimes they nauseate a wordman with their easy evasions, their slick sentiments, their ultimate futility to catch anything but the barest shadow of events, the fleeting aftertaste of emotions. But Jack, like all serious writers, knew that writing was a vow in the continuity of life, a vow that often had to be fashioned out of all the little deaths that precede the big one.

And now he's gone in October, but it's no less true.

John Clellon Holmes and Allen Ginsberg at Jack's funeral, October 24, 1969. Photo by Ann Charters.

Boulder, Colorado, July 1982. Left to right: Peter Orlovsky, Lawrence Ferlinghetti, William Burroughs, Gregory Corso, John Clellon Holmes, Allen Ginsberg, Carl Soloman, Robert Frank (seated). Photo courtesy Jerry Aronson.

ENVOI IN BOULDER

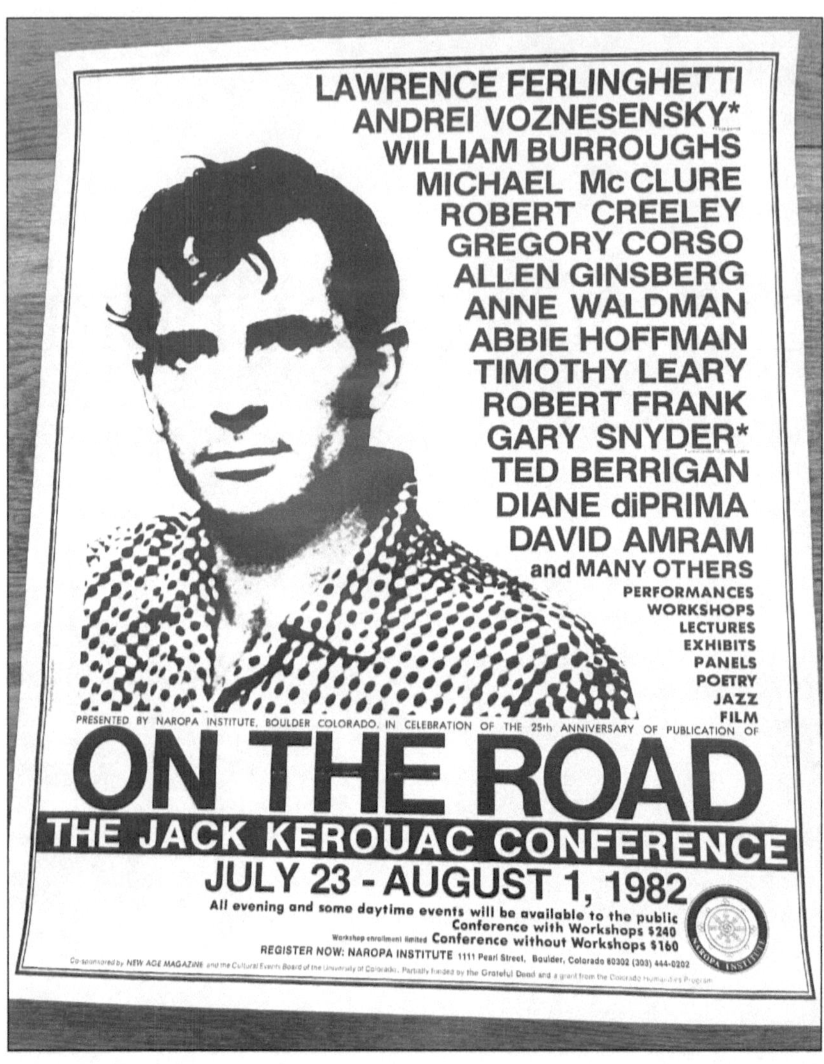

Poster from Naropa Institute's Jack Kerouac Conference to celebrate the 25th anniversary of the publication of On the Road *(Boulder, Colorado, 1982).*

IT WAS LATE JULY OF 1982. It was in Boulder, Colorado, and the mountains, the great Flatirons, were graphic and looming in the midsummer air that had an indefinable tang of new wine to it if you came from the fermenting cities of the East. Boulder was a little like Pasadena at an elevation of 5,300 feet, and I was there because the Naropa Institute was hosting a celebration of the Twenty-fifth Anniversary of the publication of *On The Road*. A lot of us, Jack Kerouac's old friends, associates and critics, were dormitoried at the Columbine Lodge of the Chautauqua compound on a tree-thick upslope on the edge of town—a plain, commodious old house with a two-storied porch, in a tangled neighborhood of run-down bungalows. All day and all night it was thronged with hangers-on, media people, and other participants in the conference who were billeted elsewhere. Our individual schedules of workshops, panels and readings were as complex as turn-of-the-century railroad timetables, and everyone was more or less continually arranging for rides to the University of Colorado Memorial Center a mile or so away, where the work sessions were held.

We had come from all over the country and from all periods of Kerouac's life, and more of us were together than had ever been in one place at one time before. We were aware that it would probably never happen again, and that this first time was to be the last time; and for some of us, though we didn't know it at that moment, it was to be a goodbye to a whole segment of our collective past, as well.

All this gave an edge of private import to the ten days we spent there that had nothing to do with the public Kerouac, or with the various lures which had attracted the hundreds of students, visitors, curiosity seekers, press, television, and film people. It kept us disturbingly rooted in the personal even as we performed as personalities. Despite the panels and the readings, the interviews and the events, the Columbine Lodge (and especially its front porch) was the true center of the conference for most of us.

On the two floors of that rambling old house, in unadorned, smallish rooms (like the rooms of a dry goods drummer's hotel in a Dreiser novel), at one time or another, were housed Gregory

The Beat Group at the Naropa Institute's Kerouac conference in Boulder, Colorado, in 1982, commemorating the 25th anniversary of On the Road.

Front row, left to right: Cross-legged on floor, Larry Fagin, Fran Landesman, Carolyn Cassady, Jay Landesman, Gerald Nicosia, Regina Weinreich, William Burroughs.

Middle row, left to right: Standing - Paul Jarvis, Anne Waldman, Lawrence Ferlinghetti, Nanda Pivano; Sitting - John Clellon Holmes, Robert Creeley, Peter Orlovsky, Allen Ginsberg, Al Aronowitz.

Back row: Clark Coolidge (between Anne Waldman and Ferlinghetti), Jack Micheline, Ann Charters, Sam Charters, Paul Krassner, Timothy Leary, Leary's friend (name unknown), man in glasses (name unknown), Abbie Hoffman.

Photo and caption courtesy Lance Gurwell.

Corso, Lawrence Ferlinghetti, Robert Creeley, Herbert Huncke, Diane di Prima, Carl Solomon, Robert Frank, Michael McClure, Abbie Hoffman, David Amram, Ted Berrigan, Jack Micheline, Ray Bremser, Ann and Sam Charters, John Tytell and Mellon, and many others.

Some of us, I'm sure, had expected, without enthusiasm, that such a situation was doomed to turn into a nonstop imbroglio of dashing egos, the sort of loft-wine-jazz-pot cabaret in which most of us had reveled in our twenties and thirties, but which is less than inviting when you are in or approaching your fifties and tend to listen for midnight when it strikes. Instead, the mood was more like that of a reunion of aging veterans, whose lives had diverged since the difficult war they had shared, but who respected one another, and who were there with a simple, common purpose that was mostly unstated during the avalanche of talk, both public and private, of those hectic ten days. We were there to attest to the validity of a literary and social movement now twenty-five or thirty years old, concretized for us in the figure of one man, who more than any other could be said to have been its prophet, its exemplar, and its most stubbornly creative spirit.

We were there to remember him, his flaws as well as his accomplishments, his follies and his genius, his influence on us as individuals, and his contribution to the direction of our national literature. We didn't talk very much about Kerouac on the porch of the Columbine Lodge; there was little outright reminiscing and no mawkish nostalgia. Jack was very dead to us, but—exhausted beyond belief by the third day, tied to an overscheduled schedule, pestered by the gnats of the media, phoning our absent families every few days—we discovered that we were still very much alive to each other. We never spoke or thought of ourselves as a hard-bitten rag-tag of lucky survivors to be listened to because of our longevity (as many who attended the conference seemed prone to do) or as a group of aging rebels who had finally matured out of their outrageousness (as the lead-ins to most of the media stories described us). There was little or none of the self-aggrandizing talk of careers and forthcoming books and internecine feuds that make most conferences of writers so wasteful of time and spirit, and inevitably leave the taste of an irrelevant debauch in the mouth as you wait in the dead deodorized air conditioning of the airport for your flight out.

In my own particular case, after a grueling year of teaching and travel that had left me worn down to the rims, I had managed to come to the conference only after postponing an overdue operation on my jaw (the first of several that would make the next four years a transition out of teaching altogether and leave me a full-time writer again), knowing that I had a date in the hospital the day after I got back to Connecticut, with at least two months of difficult recuperation and radiation to follow. As it turned out, I would never be quite the same man again, and this trip to Boulder was in the nature of a last appearance as a charter member of the so-called Beat Generation. But I hadn't come for that, nor for the modest honorarium, nor for the chance to utter any final words about my oldest, and my dearest, and my deadest friend, but because I knew I could not be anywhere else during that week as long as I could walk and talk. So I had arrived in Denver after eleven hours of the numbing tedium of planes and airports in that mood of fatalistic purpose out of which sometimes the better parts of one's nature can flourish.

When I got back to Saybrook at eleven at night almost two weeks later, I was paralyzed with weariness, oversmoked and overtalked and overbadgered, but I was strangely exhilarated too, oddly renewed, my spirit inexplicably lighter. For what had happened against all odds had been a festival of old friendships that was actually a celebration of the value of comradeliness itself, an unplanned and chaotic testament to what Allen Ginsberg called, on the first night of the conference, "tender heartedness"; this, to a crowd that clearly expected that some political or religious direction for the future might be enunciated—an extravagant expectation that was disappointed, I'm afraid. Few of us felt even

Allen Ginsberg and John Clellon Holmes. Photo courtesy Lance Gurwell.

remotely prophetic, astonished as we were to discover that the gloomy humors of our youth had left us still openhearted to life, despite everything. In all the media coverage of the many events at the conference, this single, most marvelous event of all (the possibility of person-to-person hope in a world to which the sanest collective response is despair), this event, unknown in my previous experience of such conferences, received almost no attention at all.

My most vivid memories of Boulder are not public, and have not appeared in any of the accounts of the conference that I have seen since, and perhaps were not apparent to the hundreds who attended. They were not news, they were not historic, and yet probably they constitute the final importance of the conference, not alone for me personally, but for whatever future our culture may have. The doom of nuclear disaster seemed to have paralyzed the young crowd, while as to us (alarm-ringers of the *first* nuclear generation, who had been pointing at the society's naked emperors for over a quarter of a century) the very air defied that doom, the very breath in us would not have it. The trees were in dense leaf, the big weathers of the Western sky were constantly changing, and the variety of our convergent lives (together with everything around us) seemed to murmur, "It's *not* finished." Suicidally hypnotized by technology, armed with cameras and cassette recorders as if to catch the nuance of every stray moment, the crowd was both mystified and fascinated by people as dedicated to the word as Jack had been, as we all were. Over and over, the upshot of our message was that language itself, language that was honest enough, human enough, could be the *Deed* the times demanded. Though the starkly beautiful foothills were crenellated with ominous research labs, at the Columbine Lodge, on that porch, in a motley

Gregory Corso and Allen Ginsberg. Photo courtesy Lance Gurwell.

of chairs, breakfasting on vats of coffee and baskets of croissants, we were improvising like after-hours jazz musicians, without topics or agenda, taking our choruses, building towards an upswinging ensemble riff of which the following are a few of the high notes for me—

Renewing a conversation with Carl Solomon that we had broken off the last time we saw one another thirty years before. Meeting Diane di Prima for the first time and discovering the extraordinary nurturer behind the gritty poems I had been reading for two decades. Pouring a stiff scotch for Robert Creeley when he arrived back in his room, as depleted as an actor lurching away from *Lear*, after his powerful reading. Dave Amram thrusting the recording of his *Triple Concerto for Jazz Quintet and Orchestra* at me amidst the clutter of his instruments as he rushed off to make a plane. Soft-voiced Joyce Johnson, pink and fastidious as a Dresden figurine, remembering Jack's blue eyes and brown body. Wavy Gravy and Mountain Girl (of the Grateful Dead) asking respectful questions about Jack and Rock. Impish Gregory Corso of the black-quilted vest, so proud and protective of his lovely eighteen-year-old daughter Miranda, emerging spiffed-up and poised on the night of his passionate life-affirmation of the "makers and lovers," *The Day After Humankind.* Talking with Robert Frank about my *Heidi*-sourced vision of his native Switzerland, the faint trace of a respondent smile on his deeply-seamed features as he said, "I want to film you doing that take on it,"—Robert who had peered so unblinkingly into the shudder at the heart of the American Dream.

A quiet, chatty supper with Jay and Fran Landesman on a shady residential street at John Steinbeck IV's house—John a Naropa-Buddhist, and, like them all, recognizable because they were the only people in three-piece suits; Jay saying, "Sure, I still hear from Gershon. Every month or so I get a letter from the south of France accusing me of being a fascistic dilettante. Part of the conspiracy that keeps him from finishing his autobiography," laughing over that as if amazed by the energy that kept Legman angry and had brought him (Jay) all the way here to Boulder from distant London.

Friendly remonstrances with Abbie Hoffman on the porch about the moribund political action of the sixties which he proposed to reinstitute. A few moments with Herbert Huncke in the upstairs hall one forenoon, asking about Bill Burroughs' health, and being treated to Herbert's quiet gentility, gained from years of street-wise savvy and the self-knowledge of a man who dubbed his memoirs, *Guilty of Everything.* Embracing Carolyn Cassady in the aisle of the auditorium on the very first night as if I had known her during all the thirty-five years I had only known about her, and understanding in a flash why Jack and Neal, two men of deep consequence to me who did not give their loyalties easily, had loved her so, and now, here in the West, a few miles from Neal's Denver, meeting up with each other at last. Trying to stifle my appreciative laughter at Bill Burroughs' querulous, W. C. Fieldsian half-snarl as he read from *The Place of Lost Roads* on the same platform with me, because I was afraid my mike would drown out his. Enjoying my few moments in Annie Charters' room, a scant hour or so before we were to give a panel on Jack's texts, two friends working in quick tandem, our minds running easily in the same groove. Upstairs and downstairs drinks in the boom-town Boulderado Hotel with Ferlinghetti, and di Prima, and Carolyn, and Jay and Fran, with no soppy, boozy memories befogging the pleasure. Sitting in Ken Kesey's convertible in the shadowy street outside the Columbine one late night, enthusing about Alaska and his Arkansas cousins; red-faced Ken, all grin and health, who had arrived after a forty-hour drive from Oregon, ready-to-go as always.

The "founders" dinner at Ginsberg's where Bill Burroughs, with that subtly magisterial air of a man who has gone down all the world's bleak streets, talked to me about his recent removal to

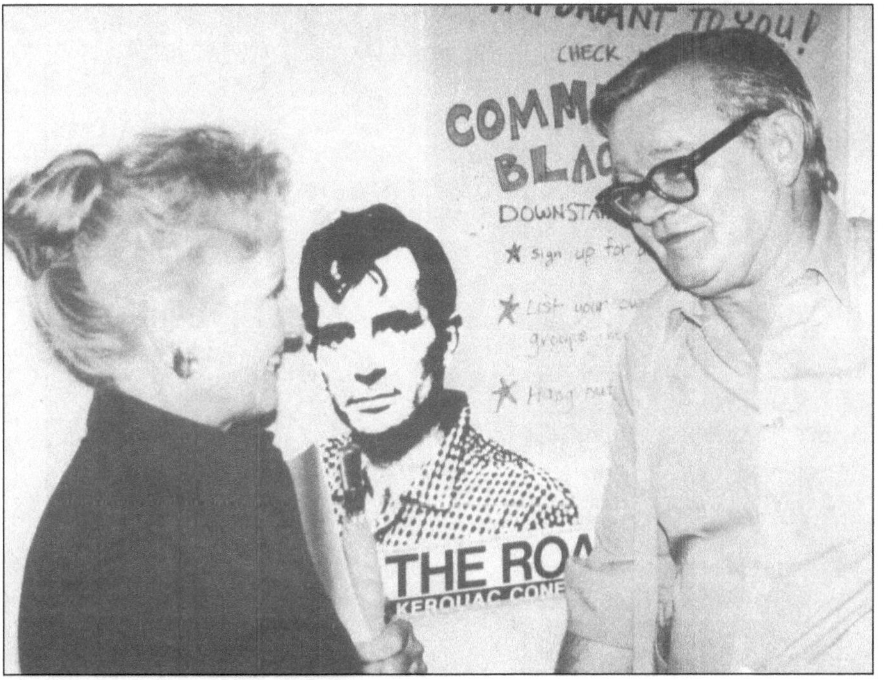

Carolyn Cassady and John Clellon Holmes. Photo by Arthur Winfield Knight.

a house in Lawrence, Kansas. Standing on Allen's porch that same evening to be photographed with Bill and Gregory and Carl and Larry and Robert and Peter Orlovsky, all of us crowded together, some of us with impulsive arms around one another. Earlier, to the sound of Peter's supper pots clanging from the kitchen, Allen saying, "I want you to hear the Rock records I'm making now, John. Maybe I'll become a b-i-g Rock star, eh?" Viewing a kinescope of Jack's appearance on the Steve Allen show in 1958, remembering with a pang that the last time I'd seen it (in Salem, Massachusetts at another Kerouac conference) Allen and I had held hands in saddened recognition of the dead flesh of our friend, as we watched his ghostly shadow move. Wanting to acknowledge in public at the last session Allen's special act of friendship in pulling off this extraordinary testimonial to Jack, but losing the opportunity in

Novelist William Burroughs. Photo courtesy Lance Gurwell.

a flurry of questions from the audience. The student in the hall who said, "All of you keep saying you never see one another—how come you seem so—so close?" And I couldn't answer him, because I didn't know. There was something about Jack that urged us all, even these years later, to give nakedly of ourselves—our secrets and our hopes. Besides, we were temporarily distracted by a new perspective on ourselves and on each other, and we were enjoying not having to explain anything for once.

So many other moments like this, literally hundreds of them, in which warm feelings, mutual respect, decent awareness of each other as separate people rather than members of a group, the absence of carping anecdote or bitchy innuendo or debilitating egowrestling, happened and continued to happen. It was mostly in idle moments that I became aware of how many years had passed.

One morning, before holding a workshop, I wandered into a large classroom on the ground floor of the Memorial Center, a room that had been converted into the conference bookstore. Tables and tables and tables of books! Hardcovers, paperbacks, chapbooks, pamphlets! Twenty-odd each by Kerouac, Ginsberg, and Burroughs. Ten of Corso's, eight of mine. More by Ferlinghetti, Creeley, McClure, Berrigan, Kesey, and half a dozen others. All in all, well over a hundred books by people who were milling around in that very building at that very moment! A whole fugitive literature!

Studying the dust jackets on the display tables was like discovering the underground, *samizdat* literature that was surfacing out of the Soviet Union just then, and realizing with astonishment how indissuadable is the human need to utter an arduouslyachieved personal truth, to somehow freeze it forever in the futurity of print, to get it beyond the reach of puritan and policeman alike, and so make good its escape from despair, edict,

Left to right: Peter Orlovsky, Al Arnowicz, Timothy Leary, Allen Ginsberg, and John Clellon Holmes. Photo courtesy Lance Gurwell.

weariness, or age. We had made something out of our rebellions and our excesses all right—But what had we thought we were redeeming with that flood of words? The validity of our experience? The fact of our existence? I couldn't remember at that moment. And there were children as well as books. Gregory had brought his dark orchid of a daughter, di Prima had brought her intelligent eight year old son. Jan Kerouac, Jack's only child, would be reading from her novel later in the week, and there were other youngsters whom I never quite identified. We had aged, we had changed. Had we changed our point of view as well? Did any single vision bind us together now as it had seemed to once? I didn't know.

One afternoon, having a hamburger steak in downtown Boulder with Gregory, who was being interviewed by someone from PBS, I caught myself looking into his intent, pugnacious face,

Poet Anne Waldman. Photo courtesy Lance Gurwell.

thrust fistlike into the cigarette smoke of the place, and remembered him thirty years before on a MacDougall Street corner when Ginsberg first introduced us—a good-looking, black-haired, young welter-weight Jimmy Cagney, all the Lower East Side in his mouth, saying, "I gave Allen some of my pomes—anyway, he *says* they're pomes—an' he's gonna tell me what's good about them." Now he was all but toothless, his gawp of mouth contorted with words, deep lines around his dark, tired eyes, a strand of silver here and there in the rumple of his hair. These years, Allen sometimes called him Gregory Jackenapes, because he got obstreperous when drunk, but he was on his best behavior this week, drinking only beer. Still, there was an edge of surfeit in him now, as if each day had gotten a little more precarious than the last, and every question that was asked of him had been answered once and for all years ago. I recognized the feeling and the look, having confronted it every morning in the mirror for longer than I cared to recall. "Anyway, Allen made me promise I'd use the bread from this gig to get me an upper plate," he said to me under his breath, "but I don't know . . . I'd like to get all my kids together for once."

One evening, at Ginsberg's house, I talked to Carl Solomon about fishing—Carl whom Allen had called an "intuitive Bronx dadaist"; Carl the frantic pogo stick yoinker of Landesman's living room in the old *Neurotica* days; big, burly Carl who had presented himself to madhouse Antonin Artaud in France and then presented himself to madhouse Rockland State Hospital in New York; Carl who wrote the densest *poete maudit* prose I knew. Now in his fifties, he still lived at home with his mother, and worked in a book store, but he spent his weekends—every weekend, rain or shine—fishing off City Island or Throgg's Neck from a rented boat. "You know, just like some *petit bourgeois* in a Renoir," he snickered. I told him that I spent most of my summers these days sitting on a shady backlawn in smalltown Connecticut, painting in acrylics from nature, trying to understand the evanescence of green things and the way of taproots with the earth.

"We got older," Carl said. "We all got older while we were paying attention to something else."

The sessions swirled on, and the good feelings held. Four women, Jack's lovers at different times of his life, worked on the same panel together with both candor and forebearance. The authors of four contending biographies did the same on another panel, treating each other's work with deference and respect. There were no scandals, no excesses of reckless libido or perilous intoxication. Our disagreements were the honest disagreements of people on the same side, and the single overriding concern of the entire conference was our feeling that our beleaguered world was not doomed after all, that our hearts were still stubbornly expectant, that we were all (in Jack's words) still making "a supplication in this dream."

His dark, frowning visage loomed over us all from the stage of the auditorium in a huge, crude painting that didn't look very much like him, and his warm voice from an old recording, asking Charlie Parker to "lay the bane off me and everybody," echoed there one morning during Sam Charters' talk on Jack's love of jazz, a talk during which I noticed a student *filming* my feet keeping time to the rhythm. The spirit of common humanity, the hope for amity and peace, all of which Jack had found so brutally lacking in the world he knew, a world in which his heart "broke in the general despair and opened up inwards to the Lord," was there in Boulder for his short life. Therein lay the celebration of that life. Therein, the ultimate testament to the man and the work.

On the last morning, I was on the porch by six thirty, having coffee by myself, and waiting for my ride into Denver and the airport. I was ready to go, to be done with it, to get back to my own life, and to whatever lay ahead, and yet—I thought of the upcoming operation for the first time in a week. I had put it out of my mind on my arrival, having decided that I wouldn't tell anyone about the prognosis, but now it gave an edge of finality to the day.

Top: Beat Generation icon Herbert Huncke and poet Diane di Prima. Photo by Arthur Winfield Knight.

Bottom: Allen Ginsberg. Photo courtesy Lance Gurwell.

I realized that I wasn't alone in my aches and pains. The nagging ailments of middle age were upon us all. Our teeth were going, our livers were damaged, the minor cancers plagued a few of us. Ginsberg had given up smoking, then taken it up, then quit again. Landesman had gotten bored with macrobiotics, and seemed a little baffled about his next move. Burroughs was rediscovering the Midwest, and Kesey was talking about maybe moving to Alaska. Gary Snyder hadn't come at all because he was erecting a meditation shack on his property outside Bolinas, and Norman Mailer hadn't come because he was still finishing his Egyptian book. I was paunchy and out of shape and some of my cells had revolted at the years of misuse. Yet the early sun splashed the street under the trees with swatches of warm light, the air smelled of dewy pavements and mountain summer. I lit a cigarette and tried to break my habit of pondering imponderables.

Part of me had never been part of the Beat phenomenon. I had always stood a little aside from it, my back to the wall and my eye on the door. By nature I was an outsider (even among outsiders), a marginal man who went off by himself to think out the meanings of things, and yet I felt an unaccountable sense of kinship with the men and women with whom I had spent the last ten days. It demanded no expression, it required no recognition. Simply, they were my crowd. I knew the things they knew. We had been shaped by the same weather in the same world. We had the same certainties and the same hopes. And suddenly I recalled having felt that same sense of fraternity years before, after my first awareness of what seemed like a new vision, and saying to Kerouac, "Something may come of this, after all."

Clearly, at the very least, it had come down to this moment in Boulder, and this long reunion. And to the questioning eyes of the students, and the flippant answers implicit in the interrogations of the media. But I was tired of all that. I was weary of relevance.

I'd apostled to the Gentiles long enough. I was aware of this particular moment as if it was a hinged door swinging outward into—I didn't know. Clearly, what we had written years before still spoke with an edge of urgency to the young. Against all odds, we had addressed our times with sufficient imaginative power to have left our fingerprints on our country and its literature. No writer could expect more.

The last three decades, like massive cliffs of glacier-ice, broke off from the main and slipped slowly backwards into the past. I was glad I'd been a part of it. I was glad it was over. Pride in my crowd, and affection for my friends, settled my stomach with the coffee.

I'd go home and get on.

Allen Ginsberg, Ken Babbs, Ken Kesey, and John Clellon Holmes. Photo by Arthur Winfield Knight.

Rick Ardinger and John Clellon Holmes, Old Saybrook, Connecticut, June 1977. Photo by Rosemary Ardinger.

PUBLISHER'S POSTSCRIPT

THOUGH MUCH HAS BEEN WRITTEN about the life and work of Jack Kerouac, no one has written more eloquently about Kerouac's innovation as a writer, or more personally about friendship and loss as John Clellon Holmes. When we approached John in 1984 about gathering these essays together for a book we published in a small edition a year later, he was thankful and flattered we would even think of doing it. The edition we produced with our grocery money at the time sold out quickly, and dog-eared copies today sell for a high price on the rare book market.

Though John's best travel, biographical, and cultural essays were reprinted in several volumes by the University of Arkansas Press around the time of his death in 1988, we thought we should offer these essays again under one cover in time for the Jack Kerouac centennial in 2022.

The changes we made to this new edition are an improved layout and design; the inclusion of the final essay (revised and re-titled by John after our 1985 edition); and the addition of some photographs. Naropa Institute's 1982 Kerouac conference in Boulder commemorating the 25th anniversary of the publication of *On the Road* brought old friends of the Beat movement together for what John knew would be the last time, and we thought that illustrating his essay "Envoi in Boulder" with images of some of those friends and Beat Generation collaborators at the conference by photographers Lance Gurwell and Arthur Winfield Knight would enhance this edition with a familial finality that John would have approved.

Though the 2022 Kerouac centennial undoubtedly will bring more scholarly analyses and perhaps yet another biography of Jack Kerouac, we thought reprinting John's personal remembrances of his dear friend was worth a go for new readers and worth a re-reading by admirers of Holmes and Kerouac and an eruptive time in 20th century American literature.

—*Rick Ardinger*
Limberlost Press

John Clellon Holmes at home in Old Saybrook, Connecticut, June 1977. Photo by Rosemary Ardinger.

ABOUT THE AUTHOR

BORN IN HOLYOKE, MASSACHUSETTS, ON March 12, 1926, John Clellon Holmes wrote stories, poems, reviews, essays, and articles that appeared in major magazines and literary journals throughout the world. He's perhaps best known for three novels—*Go* (Charles Scribner's Sons, 1952), *The Horn* (Random House, 1958), and *Get Home Free* (E. P. Dutton, 1964)—and the essay/memoir collection *Nothing More to Declare* (E.P. Dutton, 1967), a definitive work about the Beat movement and other eruptive post-World War II cultural shifts. These books were later followed by several more collections of poems and essays. His books have been translated into Danish, German, Italian, and Swedish, and have had wide circulation in the United Kingdom.

Published in 1952, *Go* is the first novel to refer to the "Beat Generation," where Jack Kerouac, Allen Ginsberg, and Neal Cassady appear as thinly disguised characters. A few years after the novel appeared, he and his wife Shirley left the hubbub of New York for the quiet of Old Saybrook, Connecticut, where they bought a ramshackle Victorian house without plumbing or heat and made it into a home to live for the rest of their lives.

Beginning in the mid-1960s, he began teaching as a visiting writer in the graduate writing programs at the Iowa Writers Workshop, Bowling Green State University, Brown University, and between 1976 and 1988 at the University of Arkansas. In 1987 and 1988, the University of Arkansas Press published three major collections of his essays—*Representative Men: The Biographical Essays, Displaced Person: The Travel Essays,* and *Passionate Opinions: The Cultural Essays.*

Over the years, his work appeared in *New York Times Magazine, Harpers, Poetry, Saturday Review, Neurotica, Partisan Review, Chicago Review, Wake, Esquire, Evergreen Review, Escapade, Nugget, Cavalier, Venture, Black Warrior Review, New Letters* (where he won the 1978 Alexander Capon Prize), *Penthouse, Playboy* (where his essays won three awards for Best Nonfiction, including one for "Gone in October" in 1973), and more.

He died of cancer at 62 on March 30, 1988.

LIMBERLOST PRESS

www.ingramcontent.com/pod-product-compliance
Lightning Source LLC
Chambersburg PA
CBHW021204110726
47900CB00002B/726

* 9 7 8 0 5 7 8 3 6 0 1 3 3 *